Customary Laws
in
Southern Sudan

Customary Laws of Dinka and Nuer

Dr. Mohamed Fadlalla

iUniverse, Inc.
New York   Bloomington

Customary Laws in Southern Sudan
Customary Laws of Dinka and Nuer

iUniverse books may be ordered through booksellers or by contacting:

iUniverse
1663 Liberty Drive
Bloomington, IN 47403
www.iuniverse.com
1-800-Authors (1-800-288-4677)

Because of the dynamic nature of the Internet, any Web addresses or links contained in this book may have changed since publication and may no longer be valid. The views expressed in this work are solely those of the author and do not necessarily reflect the views of the publisher, and the publisher hereby disclaims any responsibility for them.

ISBN: 978-1-4401-3086-1 (pbk)
ISBN: 978-1-4401-3087-8 (ebk)

Printed in the United States of America

iUniverse rev. date: 3/18/2009

PREFACE

This book is one of many books published in the last few years about the Sudan. They result from considerable international interest in the country and a desire for more information about it - this almost unknown country (despite it being geographically the largest nation in Africa). Previously the long-running civil war in southern Sudan attracted much attention globally. Lately however, the Dar Fur conflict and the atrocities associated with it, have resulted in yet more international attention. This has resulted in the international community combining to help to try to bring the fighting to an end and to provide help and assistance for the suffering population in the region.

In spite of, in general, so such bad news from Sudan, the signing of the Peace Agreement between the GOS and SPLM/A, thus ending the long lasting civil war in Southern Sudan, was one of the few items of good news from Sudan in recent years. The Comprehensive Peace Agreement is the first milestone in rebuilding the South and in commencing to restore security and order destroyed or diminished through more than thirty years of war.

LIST OF ABBREVIATIONS

ADR	Alternative Dispute Resolution
CBD	Convention on Biological Diversity
CLSC	Customary Law Steering Committee
CPA	Comprehensive Peace Agreement
DDNCDC	Daniel Deng Non-profit Consulting and Development Corporation
ECOMOG	Ceasefire Monitoring Group
ECOSOC	Economical and Social Council (UN)
ECOWAS	Economic Community of West African States
EJIL	European Journal of International Law
FCU	Field Co-ordination Unit
FMLN	Farabundo Marti National Liberation
GoS	Government of the Sudan
HRFO	Human Rights Field Officers
HRPOs	Human Rights Provincial Field Officers
IAEA	International Atomic Energy Agency
ICC	International Criminal Court
IGC	Intergovernmental Committee on Intellectual Property and Genetic Resources
INCS	Interim National Constitution of the Republic of the Sudan
IUCN	Regional Office for South America
JAM	Joint Assessment Mission
JEM	Justice and Equality Movement .

LILEAC	Legal Institutions and Law Enforcement Agencies Conference
MPIL	Max Planck Institute for International Law
NP	National Police
NRF	National Revenue Fund
NSS	National Security Service
OAGs	Other Armed Groups
PC	Police Commissioner
PCCs	Property Claims Committees
PDF	Popular Defence Force
PSC	Peace and Security Council
RCD	Reintegration Commission for Darfur
RSSI	Reform of Selected Security Institutions
SAF	Sudan Armed Forces
SAT	Security Advisory Team
SPLA	Sudanese People Liberation Army
SPLM	Sudanese People Liberation Movement
SLA	Sudan Liberation Army
SLM	Sudan Liberation Movement
SOMA	Status of Mission Agreement
SSS	State Security Service
SSU	Sudan Socialist Union
SWAN	Sudanese Women Association in Nairobi
TDRA	Transitional Darfur Regional Authority
UK	United Kingdom
UN	United Nations
UNCTAD	United Nations Conference on Trade and Development

UNESCO	United Nations Educational, Scientific and Cultural Organization
UNFF	United Nations Forum on Forests
UNI CEF	United Nations International Children's Educational Fund
UNSCR	United Nations Security Council Resolution
USA	United States of America
WB	World Bank
WHO	World Health Organization
WIPO	World Intellectual Property Organization

Contents

INTRODUCTION

Although the deeply rooted tribal and ethnic structure of Sudanese society shows the need for the adoption of a legal system, based upon customary law, in fact, and unfortunately, there has been little interest in a customary law based legal system. In spite of the fact that customary law in the Sudan, even during the Anglo- Egyptian condominium period, was recognised, however little has been achieved in developing the doctrine of customary law in the Sudan.

This led to the assumption that there was no need to develop or conduct research regarding the tenets of customary law.

There are many reasons for this; if we start with the Egyptian-Turkish colonial period, it will be clear that the Egyptian-Turkish government was more interested in the material resources of the Sudan rather than in developing its economic or legal system. The invasion of 1821 resulted in Ottoman-Egyptian rule of Sudan up until 1885; this rule was accompanied by the introduction of secular courts and a large bureaucracy. During the Turkish-Egyptian Condominium, Sudan was divided into provinces that were in turn subdivided into smaller administrative units, falling under tribal control, within which traditional tribal Sheikhs exercised administrative powers. In 1835, the first Governor General of the Sudan (Hekmdar) was appointed. In the legal sector, commercial and criminal codes were introduced in both Egypt and Sudan in 1850.

The authorities of secular courts were strengthened in favour of the rejected Sharia courts applying rules of the Hanafia School, where Sudanese are followers of the Malikia School. At the local level, sheikhs and traditional tribal chieftains assumed administrative responsibilities.[1]

In the 1850th, the pashalik revised the legal systems in Egypt and the Sudan, introducing both a commercial code and a criminal code that was administered in the secular courts. The change reduced the prestige of the qadis (Islamic judges), whose Sharia courts were confined to dealing with matters of personal status e.g. matters related to marriage, divorce and child custody. In this area, the courts lacked credibility in the eyes of Sudanese Muslims because they conducted hearings according to the Ottoman Empire's Hanafi School of law rather than the stricter Maliki School traditional in the area. The Turkish governors in Sudan encouraged the religious orthodoxy favoured in the Ottoman Empire.

The Mahdist movement started about 1880th, led by Muhammad Ahmad ibn al Sayyid Abd Allah, who became to be known as the "al-Mahdi" which means the guided one and who launched a jihad against the Egyptian-Turkish colonial government.

Even during the short period of national government under Mahdist, the government developed a legal system that was more based on Sharia rather than customary rules.

The administration in the Anglo-Egyptian colonial period tended to apply and develop a legal system based on the English common law system as adopted in India. This is not to disregard the efforts of some British administrators in Southern Sudan, who showed some understanding regarding the southern Sudanese identity and their customary laws. Those efforts resulted in the late 1920th and early 1930th, in the enactment of the previously mentioned Chiefs Courts Ordinance 1931 and The Native Courts Ordinance 1932 (amongst other enactments).[2]

The short-lived People's Local Courts Act 1977, which replaced the

Chiefs Courts Ordinance 1931, included the same purpose of its predecessor and was repealed during the civil war in 1983.

Even after independence and up until the nineties, when the Islamic-based May-laws were enacted, the adoption of a common law system in Sudan was not open to debate. The application of the Common Law System in Sudan was a de-facto matter because the vast majority of Sudanese jurists after independence were educated in the Common Law School. At time of declaring independence, Sudan had an efficient, effective and well-functioning system of justice even where claims against the Government and its departments were made, unfortunately this changed rapidly during Numeiri's regime.

Why application of Customary Law? Customary Law gives expression to the customs, beliefs and practices of ethnic group. It should be considered that Sudan as a country consists of a mixture of new-comers and ancient ethnic groups, all of them being proud of their own history and roots and still holding firm to their customary law rules as part of the above mentioned ethnic identity or origin. This fact indicates how important a role the customary rules play in every effort to unify the Sudanese. The main feature of Sudanese customary law is that its rules, with the exception of the region of Baher El Ghazal, are unwritten.

The main aim of this book is to focus on the customary rules of southern Sudan. Nevertheless, it is important to bear in mind, that all ancient Sudanese ethnic groups have their own customary rules. These include southern Sudanese tribes, the Nubian tribes in northern Sudan, the Beja and Hadandaua tribes in eastern Sudan, the Funj people of Sinnar and the Nuba, Fur and related Nilo-Saharan tribes in West Sudan.[3]

In spite of Arabic influence and the lasting impact of Islam on the Beja's lifestyle, customs and religious practices, a majority of Beja tribes still do not speak Arabic and prefer to settle their disputes according to their own customary rules. In addition, the Funj used to live in diverse groups that inhabited each Dar and have only recently regarded themselves as members of tribes. Movement from one Dar to another entailed a change in tribal identification. Tribal distinctions in these areas in modern Sudan can be traced back to this period. The mek appointed a chieftain (nazir; pl., nawazir) to govern each dar. The Nawazir administered each dur according to customary law. However, even the Arab invaders inaugurated customary law based on a tribal court system. The most significant factor involving the Guhayna group is that they comprise nomadic Arab immigrants who kept their tribal system and customary rules unimpaired from generation to next, whereas the Ga'aliìn, an older and more sedentary and therefore more heterogeneous, population settled down and mixed with indigenous people.

In southern Sudan, the Dinka have been the most populous Nilotic people, so numerous that social and political patterns vary considerably from one tribal group to another. Among the Dinka, the tribal group comprises a set of independent tribes that settled in a contiguous area. The tribe, which ranges in size from 1,000 to 25,000 members, traditionally had only two political functions. Firstly, it controlled and defended the dry season pastures of its constituent sub-tribes; secondly, if a member of the tribe killed another member, the issue would be resolved peacefully. Homicide committed by someone outside the tribe was avenged, but not by the tribe as a whole.

In post-independence Sudan, the handling of homicide as a crime against the state also made the tribe's second function irrelevant. The utilization and politicisation of ethnic groups as units of local government has supported the continuation of tribal structures into the 1990[th4]

However, the tribal chiefs lacked any traditional functions, except as respected and knowledgeable advisers to their people in personal and family matters. In the contemporary period, some attempts have been made to transform these ethnic tribal structures in order to produce a national or at least a greater sub-national identity. For instance, at the formation of the Sudanese People's Liberation Movement (SPLM), one of the main ideological tenets was the need to produce a new non-northern riverside area solidarity based on the mobilization of diverse ethnic groups in deprived areas. Although its success has been limited, to achieve this new sense of solidarity it has attempted to recruit not only southerners, but also others Sudanese ethnic groups such as the Fur, Funj, Nuba, and Beja communities. The sub-tribes were the largest significant political segments, and they were converted into sub-chiefdoms by the colonial government. Although the sub-chiefs were stripped of most of their administrative authority during the Numeiri regime, this was intended to weaken tribal structure and influence (1969-85) and replaced by loyal members of the Sudan Socialist Union, the advice of sub-chiefs was still sought on local matters.

Although a penal code and a code of criminal procedure was adopted to be applied by the state courts, the statutory law in criminal matters also guided local courts that primarily applied customary law. The code of civil justice also empowered state courts to apply customary law as appropriate to the parties concerned.

During the 1980th, this confused system of administration dissolved into virtual anarchy because of the replacement of one regime by another, civil war, and famine. In the south, however, the SPLM created new local administrative structures in areas under its control. The SPLM/A decreed that customary law should stay in force in areas under SPLM/A control, e.g. section (2) of the SPLM laws of 1984 recognized the application of the local customs of each community within the SPLA liberated areas.

In spite of SPLM/A engagement in restoring customary laws and traditional social structures in the area and its recognition of the role of local communities by involving them in playing an effective role, interference and influencing of these institutions by some SPLA leaders undermined those traditional institutions. During the 1994, (SPLM/SPLA) national convention the traditional leadership was able to forge a united front and request the political and military leaders to reassert a positive role among local communities. Measures to establish civilian, as distinct from military, administration were adopted, but the need for the movement to use the limited human and material resources available to achieve certain military and political objectives restricted its flexibility. In some instances, the differences between civil and military leaders led to further conflicts and struggles for authority.

In general, then, although severely damaged, the traditional structure of Nilotic society remained tribal and unchanged. Loyalty to one's rural ethnic community was deeply rooted and was not forgotten even by those who fled for refuge to northern urban centres.

One of the few benefits gained during the civil war by the southern Sudanese was the application of their own customary law. The southern Sudanese could make decisions relevant to their own identity - this paved the way for social and legal solidarity within a tribal group. Nevertheless, war and political conflicts alienated different tribal groups especially among the Dinka, Nuer and Shiluk tribes.

All these ethnic groups' e.g. Nubian tribes in eastern Sudan, the Funj people in central Sudan or the Fur tribes in western Sudan continued, even if in limited form to practice a tribal court system and apply customary rules especially in villages and rural areas, where the governmental court system did not reach or was ineffective.

There was a weakening in the importance of customary laws caused by the strong domination of their culture by an immigrant culture and religion (Arabic invasion) or by colonial political culture (Turkish, Egyptian or British).

Some people may see my call, for recognition of, and respect for, customary laws (as part of our Sudanese identity and part of the whole Sudanese society's ethnic structure) as tending to racial incitement. In fact, all those political and armed conflicts, lasting since the country won its independence go back to the ignorance of some self-appointed politicians, those won't recognize the diversity of Sudanese society nor accept the fact that, they will never "Arabise" or "Islamise" those who do not wish this. If those self-appointed prophets will adopt the true soul of Islam in their daily lives so that it is reflected in all what they say and do, especially in behaviours towards non-Moslem Sudanese, (e.g. stop discriminating against them, enable them to have equal chances in education and in work, treat them as equal Sudanese citizens and share with them the products of our all country and just see them as human beings - not as creatures coming from jungles and mountains), it will be enough to draw peoples attention to such a basically good and high-minded religion and the rest will follow.

The most important question is: is it really necessary to be Moslem to be recognized as a Sudanese citizen? What has Islam and the Arabic identity, language and culture to do with the Sudan as a country? These components are just part of the whole, others parts build up the existing ethnic structure of Sudan, without them as a whole, there would be no Sudan anymore. It is neither Islam nor the Arabic language which are essential for the Sudanese identity, but all those shared elements that comprise Sudanese society, whether history, customs, religions, beliefs, tribes, or other factors.[5]

Many northern Sudanese believe in the superiority of Arabic culture and make it their duty to propagate it over the whole of the Sudan. With all due respect to Arabic culture, (which is also my culture) this arrogant mode of thinking and resultant unintelligent behaviour has resulted in the long running ethnic conflicts in the Sudan. Such behaviour is a proof of the need for such people to start to inform themselves about the true basis of Islamic and Arabic culture, about which they seem to know little or nothing. It is wrong to think that all other non-Arabic Sudanese are "primitive" and without culture and they that should willingly adopt ours - otherwise we must force our culture, traditions and language on them. Such thinking indicates how little knowledge these people have, not only about their own culture but also about the country they call their homeland and about its inhabitants.

Mr. Justice Deng Biong Mijak, Chairman of the Customary Law Steering Committee described the situation in a Study for the U.S. Institute of Peace, Customary Law in the book "Crossfire of Sudan's War of Identities", by Francis M. Deng, Washington D.C., May 2005.

Some extracts are: "The war we have just ended was a cultural war.. the North thought the South was suffering from a cultural vacuum, which they called in Arabic, "el faragh al thagafy"...the system in the Sudan was trying to build itself on Arab and Islamic culture and our argument in the South is definitely that we are a people with a cultures".

The above statement reminds one of another statement by Chief Justice Ambrose Riiny Thiik "Customary law is a manifestation of our customs, social norms, beliefs and practices. It embodies much of what we have fought for these past twenty years. It is self evident that customary law will underpin our society, its legal institutions and laws for the future".

Because of the above mentioned and lasting effect of the customary legal system and rules in such an ethnically structured country like the Sudan and the traditional and ever continuing role of the customary legal system, we start this study by looking at the customary laws of the largest Southern Sudanese groups - the Dinka and Nuer.

CHAPTER I

CUSTOMARY LAW IN GENERAL

Definition of Custom

It is beyond the scope of this book to discuss the doctrine of custom and all related theories. Nevertheless, before going further into detail, some non-jurists wish to consider the meaning of custom in law or a legal custom. To explain the meaning of custom the following information is necessary. The term "custom" has come to be used in a different sense: the term custom came to be used for local customs, those of particular localities are capable of being recognized as laws even in derogation of the common law, for usages which only acquire the label "laws" when incorporated into statute or precedent, for general customs that are general custom of the realm and also for courts customs, which relate to precedents. Time is an important factor in a custom's growth since custom grows slowly.[6]

The definitions therefore are many; some describe custom as established usage, which by necessary recognition acquires the force of law.[7]

Others describe it as the established patterns of behaviour that can be objectively verified within a particular social setting, a customary law consists of those rules of custom that acquire a force of law through long practice in a given community.[8]

A custom having established usage, and fulfilling certain conditions as described by domicile rule acquires the force of law indicating a closer relation to common law system than to civil law systems, or to religiously based legal systems.[9]

Although the modern codification of civil law developed out of the customs, or customs of the Middle Ages, expressions of law that developed in particular communities, were slowly collected, and later written down by local jurists. In a study of customary law, one must bear in mind, that the custom rules comprising the law are products of necessity and thus gradually came to existence especially because of the fact, that time is a crucial element in building a corpus of customary law. This leads to another result; one cannot expect the customary law to have the complete and/or systematic structure of a modern legal system.

Customary law emerges from tribal communities' need for conflict resolution. This means that within their small community, jointly recognized, justified and accepted rules to solve given problems and settlement conflicts within this community were accepted by the majority.

A further criticism of customary laws is that, they do not cover all areas covered by modern laws. This fact, which related to the nature of customary law, does not render customary law useless or make it generally impracticable. Customary law grows just like all other legal systems and has to face new problems and provide solution for new types of conflict; it grows slowly but it still grows. On the other hand, it does not prohibit incorporation of other rules than customary rules for such cases for which customary law does not provide a remedy. A conflict situation occurs where the question: Whether to apply customary rules or non-customary rules arises.[10]

Dias explains custom as; 'When a large section of the populace is in the habit of doing a thing over a very long period, it may become necessary for the courts to take notice of it. The reaction of the people themselves may manifest itself in mere unthinking adherence to a practice, which they follow simply because it is done; or again it may show itself in a conviction that a practice should continue to be observed, because they approve of it as a model of behaviour. The more people follow a practice the greater pressure against non-conformity.[11]

According to this, custom must fulfil certain conditions to be recognized by a court of law as having the force of law. These are:

(1) The custom must be of immemorial antiquity. The onus of proving its antiquity being on the person who asserts the application of the custom. The proof becomes easier, however if its origin cannot be remembered. The burden of rebutting it lies upon the party against whom the custom is being applied.

(2) It must have been enjoyed as of right.

(3) It must be certain and precise.

(4) It must have been enjoyed continuously.

(5) It must be reasonable.

A customary law in itself is common rule that reflects the common understanding of valid, compulsory rights and obligations, those underlying social norms that have become the recognized law of a society.

In general, a custom acquires the status of law if it contains a common perception of valid legal *obligation opinio necessitates sive obligationis,* that is to say, to determine whether a custom constitutes customary law we need to question public acts, whether the related custom includes rights and obligations that define its essence. In this regard, some writers blame anthropologists for a prevailing misunderstanding related to the inaccuracies ascribed to customary rules. Anthropologists "often even when stressing the nature of custom as law, they would tend to describe it as an inflexible framework basically as it was at the time of the research. Very few anthropologists probed to determine how the customs have developed over time. The basis of customary law is not the will of the people to create the law, nor is it the conviction that the law already exists, but it is the popular consciousness that - so the law must be. Customary law does not depend on the power of the people over the law, but on the power of the law over the people."[12]

Even within contemporary legal systems, customary law is a recognized, but inferior, source of law within jurisdictions of the civil law tradition.

3

In addition, the basis of Common Law was custom. It is strictly inferior to both statutes and regulations.[13]

The modern codification of civil law developed out of the customs, or practices of the Middle Ages, expressions of law that developed in particular communities and were slowly collected and later written down by local jurists. Such customs acquired the force of law when they became the undisputed rule by which certain entitlements (rights) or obligations were regulated between members of a community. The Custom of Paris - the customary law that developed within the city of Paris - is an example of custom law. Professor John Henry Merryman from Stanford Law School summarised this in the following: "In addressing custom as a source of law within the civil law tradition, though the attention it is given in scholarly works is great, its importance is slight and decreasing.[14]

In international law, customary law refers to the Law of Nations or the legal norms that have developed through the customary exchanges between states over time, whether based on diplomacy or aggression. Essentially, legal obligations are believed to arise between states to carry out their affairs consistent with conduct accepted in the past. These customs can also change based on the acceptance or rejection by states of particular acts. Some principles of customary law have achieved the force of peremptory norms, which cannot be violated or altered except by a norm of comparable strength. These norms are said to gain their strength from universal acceptance, such as the prohibitions against genocide and slavery. Customary international law can be distinguished from treaty law, which consists of explicit agreements between nations to assume obligations. However, many treaties are attempts to codify pre-existing customary law. This being said, customary international law is often questionable as to its validity

Enacting rules for future or unforeseen cases is neither an aspect of customary law nor an expected legal activity of a tribal community.

The usual procedure preceding the birth of a customary rule is similar to the following; the occurrence of a conflict or a problem concerning various parties, elderly tribe members as well as tribal chiefs meet to debate possible solutions, the desired solution is arrived at, and, through repeatedly use, becomes a rule solve future similar conflict situations.

Modern laws and legal systems have had the same origin, but their enactment policy and procedures now work differently from those of a customary law, that is to say, a modern law provides a solution and/or punishment in advance that means, before the problem or conflict arises in contrast customary law reacts to an event. Not only the existence or non-existence of an applicable rule is the distinguishing element, but also the objective of customary law seems to be different to that of modern law. Where a customary law aims to find a settlement of which compensation may be a part, modern law, has, through the threat of punishment, an objective of providing a deterrent effect.

Certainly, compensation for injuries is also provided for in modern laws.

However, the message of a statute law, compared with conflicts settlement philosophy of customary law, sounds threatened, precautionary otherwise punishment will follow.

An opinion, proposes; "religious concepts do not provide deterrent to commit crime, it says; a man is not deterred from killing another simply because he fears spiritual contamination or the pollution of those with whom he is associated. He might do so were there no definite means by which he can remove the danger, but such means exist. What he and his kinsmen fear is the voluntary, or more probably involuntary, breach of observance which will bring them disaster in the form of natural disease *Nueer* or sterility among themselves and their cattle".[15]

This is the reason why indigenous religion generally and especially with the Dinka and Nuer is not so much a deterrent to homicide as a sanction for unacceptable modes of behaviour. It is further a sanction for the immediate confession of homicide, and this is why the Nuer rarely if ever attempt to conceal their guilt.

This maybe true regarding indigenous religions and related beliefs

However, book- religions and laws based on them do not, e.g. Islam and its Sharia.

2. Custom as a Source of Law in the Sudanese Legal System

The enactment and implementation of modern laws in Sudan started during the first period of British colonial rule. One of the first Sudanese laws was the Civil Justice Act 1900, which was followed by the Civil Law Act 1929.[16]

The above-mentioned laws were incorporated in the currently applicable Civil Justice Act 1983. Section 5 of this law specifies the proceedings in a case before a civil court. When a question regarding succession, inheritance, wills, legacies gifts marriage, divorce, family relations or the constitution of wakfs arises, in such cases, the applicable rule should be either that of Sharia , if the parties are Moslems or if marriage has been conducted according to Sharia rules. Otherwise any customary law is applicable to the parties concerned, which is not contrary to justice, equity and good conscience, and has not by this or any other enactment been altered or abolished and has not been declared void by the decision of a competent court. The above mentioned makes it clear, that a customary rule has not automatically the power of legal rule, it must fulfil some conditions to be qualified and seen as a source of a legal rule, otherwise the meaning of it will only be of traditional and of anthropological importance.[17]

In the following, we go through the conditions for recognising a custom as one of sources of laws in Sudanese legal system.[18]

3. Qualification of Custom as Source of Law

At the beginning, we have to differentiate between the existence of a custom and the recognition of it as source of law. The second point supposes definite and affirmative existence of a custom as such and so with the indiscussability of the first point study. Then the existence of such customary rules is a proven fact. The main objective of this book is to go through those existing rules in a rather comparative way starting with the difficulties they face until they recognized and become applicable and the acceptance problems raised by common law educated North Sudanese judges and the North Sudanese dominated legal system.[19]

A widespread doctrine argues that the only criterion required for a particular custom to acquire the binding force of law is for it to pass a test of reasonableness.

This is a controversial argument because 'reasonableness' is a highly subjective concept. Over time, the courts of Sudan have defined the 'reasonableness' of a custom as its conformity with 'justice, equity and good conscience.' The objection to this definition is that this allows only the judges to decide whether a custom is 'reasonable'. They in turn must make judgments about the concepts or values of a society in the light of their own community's values.[20]

The starting point, as to whether a custom can be accepted as source of law in the Sudanese legal system is given by many statutes, e.g. section 7 of the Chief's Court Ordinance provided that a Chief's Court shall administer (a) the native law and custom prevailing in the area over which the court exercises its jurisdiction provided that such native law and custom is not contrary to justice, morality or order, (b) the provision of any ordinance which the court may be authorized to administer in its warrants or regulations.[21]

The recognition of customary law was also included in The Native Courts Ordinance 32, and in section 13 of The People's Local Courts Act 1977.[22]

The above-mentioned extract indicates that the question is not whether customary rules are recognized source of law in Sudan legal system but under which conditions customary law can be applied to a dispute.

Section 5 of The Civil Justice Act includes those conditions:

A custom must fulfil following conditions before being recognize as applicable law source.

- proceedings before a civil court,

- a question regarding succession, inheritance, wills, legacies, gifts marriage, divorce, family relations or the constitution of wakfs,

- a custom applicable to the parties,

- The parties are not Moslems and marriage has not been conducted according to Sharia rules,

- The custom must not be contrary to justice,

- The custom has not been adhered or abolished by law or other enactment,

- The custom has not been declared void by the decision of a competent court.

The above-mentioned conditions can obviously be divided into external and internal conditions:

1.1. External Conditions

The first two conditions are:

(a) Custom can only be applied in proceedings before a civil court.

(b) Custom can be applied only in matters related to a question regarding succession, inheritance, wills, legacies, gifts marriage, divorce, family relations or the constitution of wakfs, are procedural conditions, which have with the kind of procedure, by which the application of a legal custom may can taken into account rather than with the legal custom in itself. The third condition in this category is related to the parties to the dispute, to rise the question of applying a customary rule, it suppose that (d) the parties are not Moslems and marriage has not been conducted according to Sharia rules.

1.2. Internal Conditions

The others four conditions are closely related with the customary law to be applied. It must have something to do with (c) a custom applicable to the parties, and such custom (f) must not be contrary to justice, (g) nor has been adhered or cancelled by law or other enactment, or has been (h) declared void by the decision of a competent court. The last condition was especially criticized because of placing the decision, to determine whether a custom is reasonable to be applied to a specific dispute or not, is in the Judges hands alone.[23]

This opinion is fully justified, taking into account that the majority of judges are mainly Northern Sudanese or Islamic oriented another problem which now losing importance was the majority of common law educated judges in Sudan and their equating of Common Law with justice, equity and good conscience. Although the blind belief in common law is dieing out with the British- educated generation of lawyers, a new "legal fanaticism" has started emerging by the enactment of the so-called May-Laws and the replacement of the blind belief in common law with Sharia, ignoring the real legal identity of a country like Sudan with a multiplicity of different religions, beliefs and ethnic groups. Not only that, but the fact is that not all Moslems in Sudan would like to be subject to doubtful Islamic related laws. Even Moslems in some regions of Sudan like Dar Fur, still have stronger ties to their customary rules than to those of common law or Numeiri's May-laws. The imposing of Sharia law on the whole of the Sudan and the Sudanese people was one of the reasons for the outbreak of the second period of civil war.

The enactment and imposition of Islamic Laws in 1983 (known as May laws) has been regarded as an ever-more dangerous threat to the application of customary law.[24]

The abolition of the May laws was one of the most important conditions of the Comprehensive Peace Agreement (CPA) of January 9th, 2005 between the Sudanese Government and the SPLM, Under chapter II that regulates power sharing under State and religion, the parties greed to the fact that Sudan is a multi cultural, multi racial, multi ethnic, multi religious, and multi lingual country and that religion should not be used as divisive factor; but the most important point was that included is the recognition of customs and beliefs as a source of moral strength and an inspiration to Sudanese people.[25]

The same wording was adopted by the draft Dar Fur Peace Agreement of Abuja between SLM/A, the JEM and GoS, furthermore article 39 provides that ethnic and cultural communities shall have the right to practice their beliefs, use their languages and develop their cultural identity. Not at least the part regulating law reform of the agreement provides for taking into consideration of recognition and application of customary rules.[26]

The above-mentioned provisions were implemented in the Interim National Constitution of the Republic of the Sudan, 2005.[27]

Besides confirming that religions, beliefs, traditions and customs are a source of moral strength and inspiration for the Sudanese people, the INCS provides that: nationally enacted legislation applicable to the Southern Sudan or States of Southern Sudan shall have as its sources of legitimacy, a popular consensus, the values and the customs of the people of the Sudan, including their traditions and religious beliefs, having regard to Sudan's diversity.[28] The INCS grants furthermore in Art. 47 that ethnic and cultural communities shall have the right to freely enjoy and develop their particular cultures; members of such communities shall have the right to practice their beliefs, use their languages, observe their religions and raise their children within the framework of their respective cultures and customs.[29]

It is unfair to compel Southern Sudanese, and other non-Muslims Sudanese (or even Muslims) to be subject to a form of law for which they have not practiced their constitutional right to choose. A compulsory application of a legal system, in this regard, Islamic law system, makes it difficult for courts to use some compromise with either customary law or any other law but Islamic law. This is not an opinion against to the application of Sharia, or an Islamic law system, but against ignoring the constitutional rights of the Sudanese people to determine the shape of the legal system they would like to subject to.

The reason why I started with a study of the Dinka and Nuer customary law systems is not that I favour them compared with other Sudanese tribes.

I regard all Sudanese as an equal people. The reasons therefore are related to the availability of study resources and materials and because of the national and international interest in the customary law systems of the Dinka and Nuer people of Sudan. It is the first study merging both in one book, this is because, as previously mentioned, because of the common ethnic origin shared between the Dinka and Nuer, and their customary law systems show some similarity. Another important factor that has facilitated this study is that their laws have been examined and recorded in far greater detail than those of any other tribe.

In addition, the right to self-determination for the people of South Sudan agreed to in the CPA agreement should pave the way for a dominant customary law system in Southern Sudan, the same steps were made concerning the Dar Fur region and it is likely that we can expect similar development in others regions of the Sudan, especially in Eastern Sudan and the Nuba Mountains area.

ROLE OF CUSTOMARY LAW IN DEVELOPMENT

Some may think holding onto customary rules hinders modernization and development, that is to say applying customary rules is a sign for rejection of change and represents underdevelopment. One may use the economical underdevelopment situation in Southern Sudan as proof for the above mentioned. I have to remark, that, having customary law or customary rules is not limited to the Dinka people of Sudan or even to Southern or Sudanese tribes only. Furthermore, economic problems and underdevelopment have been caused by other factors than the application of customary rules. Every ancient tribal group from the Indian tribes in North and South America to the Polynesians in Hawaii up to the aborigines in Australia: Each group has its own customary law rules. In Australia, customary aboriginal law has a constitutional foundation and for this reason has increasing influence. In the Scandinavian countries, customary law continues to exist and has great influence.[30]

In all those regions, which belong today to developed part of the world, customary laws still, exist, whether wholly practiced in small tribal groups or incorporated in state laws. It can be said that customary rules have a protective character rather than a negative one. Surely customary law has a protective function and protects, among others, traditional knowledge, but haven't all laws such protective functions? Protection of traditional values is a complex topic and is mostly an area of conflict between state law and customary law, taking into account that indigenous groups and local communities obviously and deeply believe that their customary law system is the most appropriate for the protection of their traditional values. At the same time, they recognize the differences as well as the complementary roles between the national law and their customary law, since the latter generally lacks adequate recognition in relation to wider national and international law.[31]

Customary laws played and still play an important role as not only as a conflict-resolving body of rules but also in managing and developing natural resources. The importance of longstanding customary rules, their role in maintaining, and contribution to natural resource development are proven facts. The best examples for such customary laws are; the Provinces of Customary Land Registration Act of Papua New Guinea, Customary Land Law in Eastern and Southern Africa, Customary Land Law in Ghana, the Saami Fisheries Customary Law and the Māori of New Zealand Fisheries Customary Law. Due to the recognition of their importance and effectiveness in ensuring sustainable development, many workshops and research groups in different countries have launched and are promoting research to achieve better legal results through incorporating the rules of customary laws into national laws.[32]

Women and Discriminatory Customary Law Rules

Customary law is not perfect nor can any other law claim perfection. The main criticism of customary law is related to its treatment of woman. Several areas of the law clearly discriminate against women or at least reflect ideas of significant inequality.

Customary law, like all ancient rules, is primarily male oriented, a woman, in spite of the recognition of her indispensable role as a wife, mother or sister, from the perspective of the male-oriented society, she occupies a subordinate role.[33]

There are many examples of discriminatory customary law rules e.g. customary law of property of the Dinka. No woman is allowed to possess land. This in spite of the fact that a man can transfer cattle and land to his wife and even female children, but those they have only the right to use, not to possess it, which means that they cannot dispose of the property without permission from the husband. A further area of the law, which appears to discriminate against women, is the issue of adultery. In the past, adultery in customary law was an offence committed by men who were made to pay compensation to the husband. Now, it seems that women are also punished for the crime with imprisonment, but for some reason they appear to be carrying the brunt of the punishment.

The rules relating to divorce are also gender biased; it is difficult for a woman to divorce even cruel husbands unless the wife's life is really threatened. Although, on the one hand, children, both males and females are at the core of the family, they represent continuity and are considered as a blessing. On the other hand, they are seen as being social insurance for their parents when they reach old age. Despite this, certain practices in traditional societies tend to violate children's rights. A further area of discrimination against females is in unequal educational opportunities that favour boys over girls; early marriage of daughters; early school leaving on account of pregnancy, favouring the father over the mother in the custody of children in the event of divorce; and female circumcision and other harmful practices.

During the long years of war, southern Sudanese women was always there to be relied on and proved their role as the backbone of the family and society, even more than the men did. Acknowledgement of this created new demands for gender equality. The role of women is seen as one of wealth-generation and distribution as well as cementing family ties through the provision of dowries, and producing children.

There is now much effort being made with a view to reforming law rules, including discrimination against woman e.g. the group discussion with Judges and Attorneys organized in Rumbek in southern Sudan in February 2005 and joined by Kuyang Anade, a Sudanese human rights activist.

Customary laws, because of their mediation nature, play a more important role than just maintaining the community social structure and healing relation between community members.[34] Sudanese customary law, in spite of the longstanding recognition of its role as one of the important sources of law in Sudan, remained largely unmodified, the only exception is the region of Baher El -Ghazal this feature make it difficult for courts to apply, for parties to provide proof of law and for jurists to commence research.

In spite of this impression, which indicates that the customary laws and practices are clearly inimical to human rights, it shows some positive practices; e.g. A married woman, especially one who has given birth to three children or more is generally regarded as beyond reproach, custom prohibits her divorce even though she might be shown to have committed a serious marital offence. Furthermore, the death of a woman or wife is a serious misfortune and she would customarily be mourned for four days whereas a man is mourned for only three days.

The above-mentioned facts indicate the importance of codifying customary law, its further development and reform and for the need to support efforts in this regard. This can be started by a process of unification of those customary laws of communities with identical or even similar customs. The successfully achievement of this step would facilitate the unifying and codifying of the customary rules of all other tribes.

The procedure for codification is simple and costs much less than other questionable projects GoS wasted tax-money in: This project has to start as soon as possible, because elderly people who are the only reliable source of not yet codified customary rules are dying out.[35]

The success to be achieved in rebuilding Southern Sudan and restoring peace in other conflicts areas of Sudan like Dar Fur and Eastern Sudan, depend hugely on how far tribal chiefs will be involved in such processes and which political role they will be given and will be allowed to play.

CHAPTER II

ETHNIC AND HISTORICAL BACK-GROUND OF THE DINKA AND NUER

There are estimated to be more than fifty separate tribal groups in southern Sudan, which each has its own discrete body of customary law, which means, that there are proximately fifty separate bodies of customary laws alone in the Southern Sudan region. A necessary introduction to the customary laws of Dinka and Nuer people is acquisition of knowledge of their tribal structure, their historical backgrounds, style of living habits and religious beliefs, since all these factors together played and still play an important rule in forming their customary rules and make it easier to understand related customary rules. Here we start with largest group.

1. The Dinka

The name "Dinka" means "people" in the Dinka language, they refer to themselves, as *Moinjaang*. The Dinka people are, like other Southern Sudanese tribes, mainly domiciled in the area south of Kosti in Bahr Al Ghazal, al Istiwa'iyah, and A'ali an Nil and are mainly concentrated in the Upper Nile province in southeast Sudan and across into southwest Ethiopia. The Dinka are widely distributed in five distinctive groups over the northern portion of the southern region, particularly in Aali an Nil and Bahr Al Ghazal in the swamplands of the Bahr El -Ghazal region of the Nile basin. Their language is also called Dinka as well as *thuongjang* and is one of the Nilotic families of languages that are closely related and are grouped by linguists into five broad families of dialects.

The five families are called Northeastern, Northwestern, Southeastern, Southwestern and South Central. Each subgroup calls its own speech by the group's name and over thirty dialects have been identified among the five language groupings, which belong to the Chari-Nile branch of the Nilo-Saharan family. They belong ethnically to the same branches of the River Lake Nilotic tribe-groups of Eastern Africa that speak Nilotic languages. Such as the Nuer and Masai They are the largest group in the south and consist of a number of smaller tribes, Dinka Malual, Twic, Rek, Ruweng, Bor, Agar, Atwot and Ngok Ablinug with estimated number up to two million. The Dinka are a black African people, differing markedly from the Arab tribes inhabiting northern Sudan, they are noted for their height (tall, thin), often reaching as much as seven feet (2.13 metres).[36]

Despite this fact, however, many other Sudanese, particularly those with lighter skin, disdain them. The Dinka are also rejected by other Sudanese people because of their leadership in the civil war that has ravaged the country for over a decade.[37] The Dinka make up a majority of the rebel army and in fact, John Garang, the rebel leader, is a Dinka. Many are Catholic and have mixed Christianity with traditional African religions, while some still follow animistic practices. The Dinka are traditionally cattle herders and value their livestock highly. For example, they give their cows names, and sometimes a herder will take the name of his favourite cow and prefer to be called by that name. Cattle among the Dinka are acquired as a gift from the father or from Kinsmen according to complicated rules. This gives the father and the elders a very strong position.

They are mainly a pastoral people, relying on cattle herding at riverside camps in the dry season and growing millet in fixed settlements during the rainy season. The Dinka's migrations are determined by the local climate, their agro-pastoral lifestyle responding to the periodic flooding and dryness of the area in which they live. They begin moving around May-June at the onset of the rainy season to their "permanent settlements of mud and thatch housing above flood level, where they plant their crops of millet and other food grains. The Dinka believe in a universal single God, whom they call *Nhialac*. Humans contact Nhialac through spiritual intermediaries and entities called *yath* and *jak*, which can be influenced by various rituals. They believe that the spirits of the departed become part of the spiritual sphere of this life. Many Dinka are Catholic and have mixed Christianity with traditional African religions, while some still follow animistic practices. The Dinka have no centralized political authority or social structure, instead Dinka comprise many independent but interlinked clans. Certain of these clans traditionally provide ritual chiefs, known as the "masters of the fishing spear", who provide leadership for the entire people. The Dinka suffered bad treatment during all of the different colonial periods as well as after independence in particular the Islamic government in Sudan has further limited their opportunities. They suffered the most loses during civil war in Sudan which has been hard on the Dinka. Most families have at least one relative who was killed while fighting against government forces. Even if a Dinka is not involved in the war, people automatically assume he is a rebel just because he is a Dinka. Renegade bands have taken some Dinka herds with no clear indication of their allegiance.

2. The Nuer

The Nuer are the next largest group found in south Sudan, numbering approximately one million and thus are only one-quarter to one-third as numerous as the Dinka. Similarly to the Dinka, they call themselves "*Naadh*" people of the people.[38]

They live mainly in the east Upper Nile Province around the junction of the Nile River with the Bahr el Ghazal and Sobat Rivers, and extending up the Sobat across the Ethiopian border. They are in the fact a confederation of tribes located in Southern Sudan and some regions of East Africa. The Nuer are divided into number of tribes; each tribe is further divided into segments and sub-segments. Collectively, the Nuer form one of the largest ethnic groups in East Africa, they share same culture with Dinka, also their languages are very close.

The Nuer language is closely related to the speech of the Dinka and Atwot. The principal tribes of the Nuer are Jikany, Gawaar and Lou.

It is unknown, why the Nuer later emerged as a separate group around the nineteenth century and pushed part of Dinka from most of their territory and absorbed the rest of them. They are a pastoral people that rely on cows for almost every aspect of their daily lives. They are one of the very few African groups that successfully fended off colonial powers in the early 1900s. Traditionally, they are cattle herders whose entire way of life revolves around their livestock. Cattle are used for payment of fines and debts and as a dowry in marriage. Children mould figures of cows out of clay, ash, wood, or any other available material. Young boys have a favourite ox that they name and treat as a pet. Although the Nuer are predominantly cattle herders, some are also engage in agriculture. They determine their calendar based on the current activity and weather conditions. The fishing season begins in December and lasts until the rain season begins in spring. The planting season follows in summer, followed by the windy season. Unfortunately, Sudan's civil war, which has lasted more than a decade, has devastated this traditional way of life and displaced many Nuer to the safety of the neighbouring country of Ethiopia or to places in northern Sudan, such as the capital city of Khartoum. Many Nuer served with the SPLA Sudanese rebel army, although some are at odds with the rebel leader, a member of the Dinka tribe. In the past, war and tribal fighting have broken out between Nuer and their Dinka neighbours.

The Nuer warriors were noted as being among the most skilled in East Africa, with weapons made of fine crafted iron. Because of their ethnic similarity to the Dinka, this makes the Dinka to favourite war object of the Nuer, that is to say, in conflicts; it is the Nuer who by tradition take the aggressive role. On the other hand such conflicts are fewer with others groups or tribes with different ethnic background like the Shilluk and Zande.[39]

They can take wives and cattle to be assimilated into their clan. Since the Nuer were so successful at fending off European powers, they spent much of their time interacting with bordering groups like those of the Dinka and Anuaks. The Nuer, being very well organized, were often able to conduct cattle raids against the Dinka, a tribe larger in population. Their traditional political organization, presented to the outside world through the ethnographic work of Evans-Pritchard, has become a classic example of an indigenous anarchist political structure without a single leader or leader group. Cattle have historically been of the highest symbolic, religious and economic value amongst the Nuer.

Cattle are particularly important in their role as dowries, - they are given by the husband's relations to his wife's relations. The Nuer are careful astronomers and have their own names for the various stars and constellations. The evening star, for example, is called "Lipai chiing"; to the Nuer, it looks like a girl in a village waiting for the moon to rise, and the name means "waiting in the village for the moon". Nuer society is patrilineal; all rights, privileges, obligations, and relationships are regulated through relatives. Marriage is one of the most important Nuer traditions and is arranged by the families of the bride and groom. The Nuer believes in monogamy, but divorce is not unheard of and is usually justified by a lack of children. If a woman does not produce children, a man may demand the return of the cattle he paid for the marriage and may return the woman to her own village. Many Nuer have remained animists or are nominal Christians. In the south, many claim to be Christian so as not to be identified as a Muslim northerner. It is very common to find a Nuer who worships a tree or some kind of animal, such as a frog. Among the Nuer, cattle raiding in the territory of neighbouring non-Nuer is an accepted practice, even promoted among the young warriors. Apart from the social instability it creates, it also makes the position of the patriarch weaker than in Dinka society. Most conflicts involve cattle and the greater part of Nuer customary law, like Dinka law, is taken up with cattle, feuds and family. In this respect, Dinka and Nuer customary law are very similar.

Because of the civil war in Southern Sudan over the past 30 years, many Nuer have emigrated to Kenya and elsewhere. Approximately 25,000 Nuer were resettled in the United States as refugees since the early 1990th, with many Nuer people now reside in Nebraska, Iowa, South Dakota, Tennessee, Georgia, and many other states.

CHAPTER III

THE SOURCES OF THE DINKA AND NUER CUSTOMARY LAWS

Just like any other legal rules, also customary law has its sources from which it was developed.

What do we mean by the source of a law?

Sources of law describe all materials and processes including court cases from which legal rules come to be developed. Such sources include constitutional, statute and case law.[40]

One may ask: why do we need to know the sources from which a law has been developed? Knowing the origin of law is always helpful to understand its meaning, objectives and aims. Whether primary, secondary or even tertiary, such sources are indispensable in conducting effective research into a law.

1. Sources of Dinka Customary Law

Dinka law has, compared with others laws, four sources, those are:

(1) Practice, (2) judicial decisions, (3) religious beliefs, and (4) principles of morality.

1.1. Practice as Source of Customary Legal Rule

A custom grows out of repeated practice, not a practice of an individual or of a small group, but of the community; the case, on the other hand indicates the importance and suitability of a practice to deal with a certain situation. The practice in the above-mentioned meaning is the first and most important source of a customary law.

Very decidable is the psychological or subjective belief, that such behaviour has the power of law or the existence of a similar situation of *opinio juris* in the international customary law.

Unlike the common law, Dinka customary law does not requires a fixed period of time, from which an immemorial antiquity of a custom should start, but it supposes it as a fact unless the opposite can be proved.[41]

Such a point of view is essential for elevating a custom to the position of being a legal rule. The above-mentioned start point does neither prevent nor ignore the right of a party in a conflict to raise doubts, as to the immemorial antiquity of custom or its validity before a Dinka court. However, usually in such case of given fact, the burden of proof lies on the party claiming the opposite, but in fact and according to a Dinka court procedure, raising such doubt will be enough to oblige members of the court to prove that relevant custom has been applied as law for long time.[42]

1.2. Decisions of Courts and Case Law

Courts decisions or judicial precedents refer to the way in which the law is made and amended through the decisions of judges. In the common law system, court decisions are described as judge-made- law or law developed through decisions by judges necessary to decide cases brought before them. The importance of court decisions in the doctrine of case law in developing law is not only limited to the common-law system but has same meaning in civil law system as well in the customary law development process.

The same can be said about Dinka customary law, although it has no formal case law system in the modern sense, courts decisions played and play an important role and have made a remarkable contribution to its development. Judicial decisions are likely to be kept in their memory by the chiefs to be later applied in similar cases, it is unclear, whether such memory included only *ratio decidendi* or also *obiter dictum*.

A greater contribution to the development of case law has been achieved by the enactment of the previously mentioned Chiefs' Courts Ordinance 1931, which paved the way for building Chiefs' Courts and enabled the exchange of judicial views and enabled the holding of conferences on border disputes.

As previously mentioned, the first laws addressing the implication of the customary laws were the Civil Justice Ordinance 1929 and the Chiefs' Courts Ordinance 1931. The first of these laws is the predecessor to the current section 5 of the New Sudan's Civil Procedure Act 2003. The second law was a novel development in that it formally recognized customary Chief's legal authority to exercise customary jurisdiction in their traditional tribal areas. The Chiefs' Court Ordinance 1931 was the most significant milestone in Sudanese legal history in the north as well as in the south of the country.

The above-mentioned law although it underlined loyalty to the colonial administration but on the other side, it recognized and strengthened the role of tribal chiefs. In some ways, the Chiefs' Courts Ordinance 1931 recognized the tribal structure of Sudanese society and the importance and effectiveness of customary rules.

After independence, the same recognition as to customary laws in Southern Sudan was stressed by section 12 of The People's Local Courts Act 1977 that repealed the Chiefs' Courts Ordinance 1931. The so-called May- laws enacted in 1983 were not applied in areas under the control of SPLA/M during the second period of civil war.

1.3. Religious Beliefs as Source of Law

Religious belief describes usually a mental state in which faith is placed in a creed. Religion can on the other side be the main source of a legal system, the best-known example of which is the Sharia. The role of religious beliefs as source of law is not limited to religion-based legal systems but plays an important role in customary laws like Dinka customary law. This can be seen in rules related to the prohibition of incest and adultery. Such beliefs range from belief embodied on a person, which believed to be God's reprehensive like the medicine man, named *Banybirth* in the Dinka language.[43]

The decisions of the *Banybirth* are of great religious meaning, regardless whether they made within or outside a court.[44]

1.4. Morality as a Source of Law

Morality means a code of conduct held to be authoritative in matters of right and wrong. Moral values are usually created by and defined by society, philosophy, religion, or the individual conscience. That means, morality creates rules, which govern the conduct of a society, it has the duty to incorporate them in enforceable legal provisions. Morality in this sense describes how people should behave; the law is concerned with should be dome when they do not behave correctly. However, the inseparability of law and morality is beyond the scope of this study - we are only interested in morality as source of the Dinka customary law. In the Dinka customary law like in other laws, morality is the source of many prohibitions, e.g. rules forbidding murder, stealing, etc have their original principles of morality as well in religion.

2. Sources of Nuer Customary Law

The fact that Dinka and Nuer and their customary rules as well have same origin and share similar factors let one suppose the same regarding the sources of their customary rules. Especially, religious belief is deeply rooted in the Nuer as well. The basic of their religious belief is a concept named *Kwoth*.[45]

In general, Nuer customary law has four primary sources:

These are: Firstly, the Practice: which can be described as a custom or tradition that has been repeated over many generations at the community rather than individual level. Secondly, court decisions: including, beside customary courts also statutory courts with jurisdiction to decide on matters of customary law. Thirdly, religious beliefs which definitely have a given role in the treatment of matters such as incest and adultery. Fourthly principles of morality.[46]

CHAPTER IV

THE STRUCTURE OF DINKA AND NUER CUSTOMARY LAWS

It is not to be expected that customary law will have the same structure and divisions as is seen in modern legal systems, in Sudanese customary law just as in other customary legal systems or even in religiously based legal systems, it is difficult to clearly distinguish between criminal and civil matters The division of laws into private and public, material and procedural or national and international, into civil and criminal, is one of the aspects of modern law systems. Modern law systems have developed to govern a larger community with a far more complex and multi-layered structure that that of a tribal group. That is to say, each legal system is as complicated as is the society it has to govern. In general, customary laws have the tendency combine the treatment of civil and criminal laws.[47]

Another feature, which relates to a tribal community rather than to customary law per se is that there is a lack of law enforcement and crime prevention agencies. Officials with a mission to carry out crime prevention and law enforcement duties are not be necessary in a small tribal community where crimes rarely take place. In such cases where decisions of tribal chiefs are to be enforced there is always enough volunteers those would carry this duty in accordance with group-solidarity principle. This fact, the non-existence of law enforcement agencies and related justice institutions within the tribal community leads to a restricted range of penalties for transgressions of whatever kind (criminal or civil) - principally to material compensation as a penalty, as there is neither imprisonment nor prison or any kind of physical penalty.[48]

However, even within tribal communities, changes are taking place in the direction of a developed and larger tribal community. This fact demonstrates the need for similar developments in the sector of customary law enforcement.

The long civil war and its aftermath, large-scale immigration and the long period of lawlessness contributed to widespread serious crimes, which only can be combated through well-functioning law enforcement departments.

This is not to deny the role of SPLM/A leaders in restoring order within areas under their command. The responsibilities of the SPLA field commanders often involved much more than combat. Over time, it took on the task of maintaining law and order in the community - to the satisfaction of the local population.[49]

The war destroyed, among many other things, also the infrastructure of the judiciary, police and prison services. During the long period of civil war, the few jurists, who had not been killed or arrested emigrated, for others it was not possible to start or continue legal education during the war. There is an immediate and pressing need for trained judges, lawyers and trained personal in all law enforcement departments.[50]

The situation detailed above does not mean that customary law lacks regulations for the tribal legal matters in question. The customary laws of the Dinka and Nuer comprise, just like other legal systems, rules dealing with personal matters, which modern legal systems classify as family law matters e.g. Marriage, divorce, and child custody as well as rules for matters classified under matters of criminal law in modern legal systems that include offences like homicide. The customary law also includes rules that regulate similar property matters, not all topics regulated by state law but some of them e.g. disputes related to the ownership, possession, transfer and tracing (etc) of property. In general, a legal owner of property, except in certain circumstances, is authorised to reclaim his stolen property from the hands of the holder who either acquired it unlawfully or in good faith provided the relationship for which it was so acquired has ceased to exist. Nevertheless, there are exceptions to the right of reclaiming property by the owner, one of which is the rights of the innocent third party or where the property in dispute was acquired by the defendant in settlement of a debt or as compensation. The finder of lost property acquires its possession only as a trustee. He can acquire its ownership where a true owner cannot be discovered after the expiration of a reasonable period. If the legal possessor appears even after the above-mentioned period has expired, the finder will have to return it to legal owner. The most import issues related to property regulated by customary law are related to livestock (cattle) and land property. Land property, the individual's right to land as a community member, as well as property acquired by individual members of the community for their homesteads and marked off agricultural land, all these topics are administered on behalf of members of the community by the chiefs in the Community.[51]

Customary law specifies reserved land which is excluded from individual ownership to be used by all members of tribal community, this reserved land can also be used by individual member from tribal community, but without any right to claim ownership on it nor to prevent or forbid others community members (foreigners are excluded) from using or having access to this land. The above-mentioned land subject to common community use is not limited to agricultural land; it can also include areas like forests, fishing- waters, and pastureland.

Trading activities take place between tribal members themselves as well as with outsiders. Customary laws include rules to regulate these activities and commercial transfer of goods possession that usually takes the form of barter.[52]

In the criminal sector, customary law do not draw clear distinction between criminal and civil matters - some rules belong to both categories. These include compensation for homicide cases and sexual offences.

This fact can be seen in the similarities between penalties and compensations. These similarities between criminal and civil matters extend to the related procedures, which are for both matters the same.

As previously mentioned the main function of customary Law is not punishment but arriving at a settlement or as John Wuol Makec stated: "customary Law is not retributive but is concerned with maintenance of social balance or maintenance of status quo"

Customary law mainly tends to create a social balance within the tribal community and even with neighbouring tribes, but laws in general also have a deterrent aspect. Customary law seeks to achieve a deterrent effect through increasing the compensation payable in cases, where a type of crime e.g. theft and adultery, has become more prevalent.[53]

Customary laws, in this regard, of the Dinka and Nuer, are applied in a specific territory where they are administered under a statutory law, for example under the Restatement of the Bahr El -Ghazal Region Customary Law (Amended) Act, 1984.[54]

The study of Dinka and Nuer customary laws in the following chapter will start with rules related to family matters within customary law and then with criminal law matters.

CHAPTER V

CUSTOMARY FAMILY LAW

Definition and scope of family law

Family law is the body of legal rules regulating family relationships, it deals with such areas as: marriage, separation, divorce, adoption, child custody and visiting rights, children's rights, child support, spouse support, separation agreements, civilian and military divorce (dissolution of marriage), marital property division, elder law matters, estate planning, estates and trusts, wills and contesting of wills, probate, insurance, cohabitation agreements, pre-marital agreements and other legal issues pertinent to the family. The part of Dinka customary law dealing with family matters is known as *Lôônge- Kôôcē Ruāt*.

According to the classification adopted by the Re-statement of the Baher El- Ghazal Region Customary Law Act, 1984 we start the study with rules as to marriage:

1. Dinka Customary Marriage

Marriage is the basis for forming a family, especially in a tribal community, which refers to marriage as: *Ruāi*. The legal definition of marriage is to be found in Sec. 20 the Re-statement of the Baher El- Ghazal Region Customary Law Act, 1984: Union between one man or his successor and one woman or more women for their lives for the purpose of sexual cohabitation. Procreation of the young and maintenance of the homestead, provided that such a union may take place between one barren or childless woman and another for whom male consorts are provided: provided also that such union may take place between a deceased male person and one or more women through his successor.

The above-mentioned definition emphasise many aspects of Dinka customary marriage rules and customs, those can be summarized in the following features:

A polygamy feature: according to section 19 of the Dinka Customary Law a Dinka man has the right to enter into marriage relation(s) (union) with one or many women.

The definition does not explain, whether there should be a limitation on the number of women a man is allowed to marry.[55]

Dinka customary law does not includes any legal prohibition as to polygamy. The only obstacle that restricts polygamy can be the financial situation of the man - which can be seen as temporary obstacle. Polygamy is wide spread, especially in customary law areas but it is also known in other legal systems like Sharia whether in African or in other countries. On the other hand, economical factors, the higher expenses of modern life and female emancipation are having a strong influence in gradually rooting out polygamy.[56]

Inheritability of marriage: the expression (...between one man or his successor ....) indicates another special aspect of marriage in Dinka customary law as an exception from the principle of marriage as a personally binding, provided also that such union may take place between a deceased male person and one or more women through his successor.

This demonstrates that the coming together of the spouses' families is an important part of the wide scope of Dinka marriage. It worth mentioning, that for the validity and legality of marriage according to Dinka customary law, neither registration nor other formalities like the issuing of a marriage certificate are necessary.[57]

The description of marriage as "binding for life" is a condition that belongs to the nature of this relation and usually included in all laws.

The difference concerning Dinka customary marriage is that the afore-mentioned union refers to the lives of the married women but not to the lives of the men.

That is to say, the marriage the relationship ends when the wife dies, but not when the husband dies. Section 38 of Dinka Customary Law specifies the case when death may terminate a marriage relationship. It states:: Death of the wife may terminate the marriage relations between the spouses but the death of the husband has no such effect.

In the Case of death of one or both spouses "Parents" the continuity of marriage is emphasized by family-ties embodied in the children descended from marriage-relationship. Those children are the link between both families. This also why the marriage–relationship or "union" is to be regarded as not having achieved its objective, when the couple remain childless.

As previously mentioned the role of women is seen as one of wealth-generation and distribution as well as cementing family ties through 'dowry', and producing children. Since the value of women is associated with childbearing, "a barren woman may 'marry' another woman to beget children in the name of her deceased husband. Someone would then be identified within the family to live with the woman so married as husband and wife. The 'woman-husband' retains all the spousal rights including divorce and chastisement minus of course, the conjugal rights. This kind of custom creates a number of problems for the 'wife' whose loyalty has to be shared between the woman-husband and the man actually cohabiting with her.[58]

A specific feature of Dinka customary marriage is the case, when an unmarried man dies or when a married man dies before fathering children. In case of dying unmarried, a representative of the deceased, who is a "successor" named by the family of the deceased as trustee, will have to marry a woman as a proxy for the deceased. Although the whole family of the dead is involved in arranging this marriage, the responsibility for raising the children lies with the successor alone. In the case of the death of a childless married man, it will be the obligation of successor to produce children with the wife of the deceased. It worth mentioning, that the responsibility, obligations and role of procreator towards the resulting children and the deceased's wife seem to be identical with those of the real farther (the deceased) unless his role is subject to some limitations. This is usually the case, if relationship between the deceased and his successor is of some distance. The closest kinsman of the deceased is appointed to take care of the family and property of the deceased.

This also should be the case, when the successor "procreator" neglects, badly treats the deceased's family and property or intends to take the deceased 's wife as his own, the closest kinsman or even the deceased's wife herself can replace the successor "procreator" - either by another kinsman of the deceased or someone else altogether.[59]

Regarding the above, Dinka marriage can be divided in the following categories:

1.1. Single Simple Marriage

This is the kind of marriage, (when a Dinka man marries a Dinka woman), which refers to the union between one man and one woman.

1.2. Polygamous Marriage

This is the case, when a Dinka-man marriage two or more Dinka women.

Whether the bridegroom should enter into a polygamous marriage relationship with two or more women in one ceremony or separated ceremonies, has no importance, The simple fact, that a marriageable Dinka-man is willing to marry one or more women, constitutes the pre-condition for a polygamous marriage.

It is worth-mentioning, that polygamy is not only practiced by the Dinka alone, in such communities, where the traditional marriage practices still prevail, being married to more than one woman is a symbol of wealth, success and social and political importance.

1.3. Marriage by a deceased kinsman

When a Dinka man dies before being able to marry, his kinsfolk are obliged to arrange a marriage for him, by which, one of his kinsmen, usually a brother, will marry a woman as a proxy for him and procreate children in the name of his dead brother or kinsman. This kind of marriage among the Dinka is similar to the "ghost-marriage" of the Nuer (as will be explained below).

2. Conditions for the validity of a Marriage

The following conditions are necessary for a marriage to be valid, these are: consent, maturity, provision of a dowry, undergoing a marriage ceremony. A detailed discussion of each condition follows:

2.1. Consent

Consent is a basic condition in every contractual relation and so it is in marriage relations. Consent is known as "*Gēm/Gam*" in Dinka language and defined in section 12(i) of the Restatement of the Baher el- Ghazal Region Customary Act 1984 The only consent which is material for the conclusion of a valid marriage is that of the spouses, parents, brothers and close paternal uncles in that order of importance".[60]

The above extract emphasizes the indispensable importance of consent for the validity of marriage. The order in which the expression of such consent should be requested to have the legal effect for the marriage to become valid is that of parties to marriage, parents, of brothers or of close paternal uncles in order of closest relationship or importance. Consent in this order is requested on both sides, by the kinsmen of the man as well as by the kinsmen of the woman.

Unlike consent in other contractual relations, it happens that the consent of the spouses come to be ignored, e.g. in cases of marriage for tribal political or economical interests.[61]

Such a situation although it does not prevent the marriage, even without the consent of their families, but can leads to some complications if one or both families refuse to ratify this marriage. The marriage can only be seen as union between spouses' themselves but not between their families but without producing legal effects.[62]

2.2. Maturity

Capacity is a condition known in all marriage laws and laws of contracts. Capacity is called *Dĭt* in the Dinka language and refers the necessary maturity for marriage. According to section 21(a), no marriage shall be consummated between a boy and girl until both of them have attained maturity. Unlike others marriage laws, which stipulate a minimum age or even full legal age, maturity in Dinka customary law is determined only by certain physical features. . Paragraph (b) of section 21 describes requisite physical features: for a girl, the beginning of maturity is marked by the first menstrual period, while for the boy, it is marked by certain physical changes, such as the voice breaking, growth of hair in the arm-pits or genital areas or by traditional marks designed to mark the end of the period of boyhood.[63]

2.3. The Dowry

Also known as, bridewealth or bride-gift is known in many customary and religious based laws. The dowry, knwon as *Hok- Thieek* in Dinka language is similar to the *Maher* or bride-gift in Islamic marriage. It is the gift paid by the groom and/or his family to the bride and/or her family.[64]

The contents of which differ from one society to another. Traditionally the bride gift in a Dinka marriage or in marriage between Dinka and others stockbreeder tribes is to be paid in cattle -otherwise the marriage would not be deemed as valid. Money and others gifts do not include cattle gifts made by the groom's or his family before or at the time of engagement - they are not regarded as part of the dowry. In some rare cases, where groom neither possesses cattle nor is able to provide a dowry in purchased cattle, the dowry can also be in monetary form.

As soon as there is consent for the marriage, both families gather to discuss the appropriate amount of cattle to be the dowry.

The factors playing a role in determining the number of cattle are e.g. the social status of family, the groom's finical status and that of his family and personal elements specified to the bride herself e.g. character and behaviour. One must remember that the dowry would be gathered collectively by of all members of the kinship group to enable the relative to contract the marriage.

2.4. Marriage Ceremony

The preparations for wedding- ceremony start as soon as the agreed to amount of cattle has been delivered to the bride's family. The ceremony is terminated by delivering the wife to her husband.

2.5 Final Remarks on Dinka Marriage

From the previously mentioned features of Dinka's marriage compared to the summary (below) of Nuer marriage, many similarities will be seen. Before coming to an end of this description of Dinka marriage, and because of the discussion in the western community about the meaning of dowry and the widespread misunderstanding of it as kind of slavery or as custom that discriminates woman I would like to explain the meaning, background and purpose of dowry:

Dowry is sought to supply a material symbol, which legalizes the union of man and woman and establishes the legitimacy of the children of the union and their lawful inheritance.

Dowry provides emphasis and legality to the conventions and patterns of behaviour and the reciprocal obligations, which are raised between the kinship groups concerned, and must be, observed if the union is to be successful.

Dowry also provides stability to the union, particularly in the initial stages when it has not been confirmed and fortified by the birth of children who will subsequently form a link between the lineages concerned.

Dowry has also the function to guarantee correct and good behaviour of wife in the future within her new family- otherwise incorrect behaviour can lead to the dissolving of the marriage with the obligation of the returning the dowry. On the other side, the husband is also obliged to treat his wife well, otherwise, he loses his dowry, if she leaves him.

3. Nuer Customary Marriage

In contrast to Dinka marriage, there are different forms of marriages or more exactly, forms of domestic union according to Nuer customary law. The main difference lies on whether a marriage has a legal basis or not. The deciding factor of legality of such marriage i.e. whether a marriage has a legal basis or not, is that of cattle transfer. The marriage types are detailed in the following:

3.1. Single Legal Marriage

This form of marriage takes place through the union between man and woman after paying a dowry. It corresponds in form and procedure with the previously mentioned form of marriage among the Dinka.

3.2. Ghost Marriage

In fact, the marriage itself has nothing to do with ghosts, the name "ghost marriage" related to the fact, that entering such a marriage should be in the name of a dead relative, who died before being able to marry or married but has not any successor male child/children.

It is the duty of the relatives of the deceased to fulfil this binding mutual kinship obligation. This obligation lies usually upon the brother of the deceased, the non-performance of which leads to restlessness of the dead and sets a curse upon his kinship. Because of fear of the curse and to enable the deceased to rest in peace, this obligation is always carried out, especially when sufficient cattle are available to pay a dowry.[65]

Consequently, ghost marriage is distinguished from simple legal marriage in the following ways:

-       The marriage is conducted in the name of the dead relative, for his well being and on his behalf, i.e. the ritual process of marriage is performed in his name, the dowry is paid on his behalf, and the children will carry his name.

- The relative to marry in the name of his dead relative is obliged to fulfil all the obligations as a husband, and as the physiological father of the children, i.e. he is a husband, and farther in practical sense but not in the legal one, that is the dead relative.

- The ghost wife *ciek jooka,* is theoretically, on the one hand, has ghost-marriage relationship respectively ghost-marriage with the dead and, on the other hand has simple marriage relationship with the relative.

3.3. Levirate Marriage

Although, in this case, the widow of a dead kinsman continue to have a marriage relation with one or all kinsmen, but no marriage ceremony takes place nor is it necessary. It is expected that, when the relative dies, his wife widow" who legally continues to be seen as his wife, will stay with his relatives group because of solidarity principle in tribal kinship communities and because of the role of the deceased's relatives in providing a dowry.

The levirate is a legal union and, in some cases, a relative cohabiting with the widow, although rarely permitted, may demand her divorce from his dead relative. However, levirate is not to be mixed up with ghost marriage. By ghost marriage, the vicarious husband as legal representative of the dead man actually marries the widow in a marriage ceremony preceded by the payment of a dowry.[66]

In most cases, the widow remains in the kinship group of her dead husband, mostly with his brother or even with other categories of relatives, and continues bearing children in his name, but for the benefits of the entire kinship group, where they all benefit from the domestic and economic services of the widow as well as those of the children.

It is important to mention again, that the cohabiting of the widow with a relative of her dead husband is neither ghost-marriage nor constitutes any kind of marriage relationship. Moreover, should the widow cohabit with anyone outside the kinship group; the kinship group has the right to demand compensation for adultery.[67]

4. Conditions for Nuer Marriage

Insofar that there is no codification of Nuer marriage law, and regarding the similarity in customs and tribal practices with their neighbours the Dinka, almost all conditions mentioned regarding Dinka customary law can also be applied to Nuer customary law.

In the following, only the features that differ in respect of Nuer customary law will be discussed.

4. 1. Consent to Marriage

In the case of a Nuer marriage, first, acceptance must be shown by Nuer girl to an interested Nuer man. Then, it is the Nuer girl, who has to inform her family. This step assumes she knows that the bridegroom has enough cattle for immediate payment of a dowry.

In spite of the first consent and the step made by the Nuer girl, her legal representative in her family or kinship group (farther, brother, uncle) still can refuse to agree to the marriage for any reason, e.g. because of a blood feud between the two families (*teke riem kamdien*).

In such cases, her kinship group can forbid her to meet with the Nuer man in question. Otherwise, if there is no objection from either side, the Nuer girl is allowed to meet her bridegroom. Then meeting take place in the neutral home of an outside person, often a friend of the bridegroom. This meeting is called *luom nyal* and means courting the girl. At the meeting, friends of both bride and bridegroom come together and a representative of the bridegroom and a representative of the bride perform a ceremony- mentioning the good character of each and praising him/her. After the *luom nyal*, which is not official engagement, a second meeting take place, called *thiec nyal* and meaning "asking for the girl".

This *thiec nyal* meeting is the first coming-together of the parents or representatives of both bride and bridegroom. Although the *thiec nyal* is official meeting towards concluding the marriage but it dose compel to perform the marriage ceremony.

The delivery of the dowry then takes place after consent of all parties as to the marriage as well to the amount of dowry have been reached.[68]

4.2. Maturity

Since the main objective of marriage, (especially among the Nuer) is to have children, reaching the right age by both boy and girl is an essential pre-condition for such a union. The same rules relating to this point under Dinka marriage are applied in regard of Nuer marriage. Usually the previously mentioned *twoc* ceremony will not take place before the girl has reached puberty. The Nuer describe it in these terms: the girl is ready for the *muot*, which actually means shaving, or *muot nyal* means shaving of the bride.[69]

4.3. Dowries

The dowry "*Thakha*", is usually delivered in the form of cattle. It is also a pre-condition for a Nuer marriage, as we have seen. The number of cattle agreed to by the *thiec nyal* is to be delivered in a further ceremony called *twoc ghok*, which means "introduction of cattle". Although there is no fixed time limit for the *twoc ghok* ceremony to take place, both parties are keen that it takes place as soon as possible. This, in contrast to the foregoing ones, is a public ceremony. It is expected that all kin of bridegroom are present, especially those contributed to provide the dowry.

On the other side are also all the kin of the bride who will be present to receive their part of the dowry.

4.4. Marriage Ceremony

A marriage ceremony is a traditional ritual in a tribal community

Generally, one can say, there is no marriage without a ceremony

The marriage ceremony consists of many stages, the most important of which is the shaving of the bride. The marriage ceremony starts with the loosening of the rope, which Nuer called it as *loiny deb*. The procedure is: the bridegroom, dressed in cat skin goes with his fellow "friends" and others youths of his age to the bride's home to ask for her public consent. They spend the day and the whole of the night in conversion and singing. Although sexual practices may come to take place between the bride and groom- these, occur without consummation. The next morning the bridegroom addresses the bride's mother on the subject of muot, which is usually, follow this. The bride's mother usually gives her consent due to the promise of special presents called *nyin daba*.[70]

With the bride's mother showing consent, the ritual of loosening the rope follows, which symbolizes the bride's release from her father's household. In the same evening, the ritual of *noong nyal* or the bringing of the bride to the bridegroom home take place. In preparation for this, representatives of the bridegroom inform the bride's family that they are ready for them. The bride is then assisted into the wedding hut and the bridegroom goes in after her. The previously mentioned ritual of *muot nyal* or the shaving of the bride follows the next day, on which the bride is usually taken in the morning to the home of some unrelated person nearby, but is brought back to the bridegroom's home towards evening.

Finally, it needs to be remarked that the indigenous institution of marriage of African tribes seems to be strange and obscure for outsiders. Unless it can be studied as part of the whole couture and customs, or according to some western observer:

The indigenous institution of marriage can only be understood if it is viewed as integrated part of this kinship system as a whole. It here, for example, that we find the key to certain customs which obviously, presupposes a conception of marriage as a transaction giving rise to reciprocal rights and obligations between two groups of kinsmen and binding those groups together in a relationship as spouses. This principle of continuing relationship is closely connected too with the institution of the dowry, which collected collectively by the kinship and it finds expression for example in the levirate that supposes the continuance of the marriage relationship between the widow and one of the deceased's kinsmen. .

5. Dinka Divorce

Without going deeply into the discussion, as to which description: divorce or dissolution is more relevant to describe ending Dinka marriage, we would mention that the expression in the Dinka language related to divorce - *puoke-ruai* or *dake- ruai* has wide scope and can also be understood in the sense of meaning the dissolution of a marriage.[71]

The expression puokē-ruāi describes the situation in which a marriage is to be completely terminated, regardless of the reasons therefore.[72]

According to section 35 of the Restatement of the Baher El Ghazal Region Customary Law Act 1984, a valid divorce shall always be granted by the Court with the consent of all or a majority of interested parties to the marriage contract. The puokē- ruāi in this sense is judicial divorce and deviates from the more common private divorce which is wide spread in Sudan especially among Moslems. The main features characterizing the puokē- ruāi divorce is that it can only take place in a court, the agreement of parties to whether conditions therefore are fulfilled or not plays no role, the decision of the court regarding grant of divorce is final one. On the other hand, if the parties agreed to a private divorce without involvement of the court, although this divorce is illegal, no court can compel parties to continue a marriage relationship. In many cases, the parties may be unable to settle their rights or claims when the divorce take place out of the court and they may need court involvement later to settle their dispute.

5.1. Why Court Divorce?

There are some reasons justifying why the lawmakers have provided for divorce to take place before a court:

- The law-maker's objective in requiring a court decision for a valid divorce serves to make it difficult rather than easy to divorce – thus supporting the retention of family ties.

- The second reason is to guarantee publicity of such a divorce and make it known to every interested person. A court decided and documented divorce is important and offers protection, especially in such cases, where one may be accused of adultery with divorced woman.

- Conducting a divorce or puokē-ruāi before a court enables community members and the public to find out, who is to blame for the dispute and for the resulting divorce. The party to the dispute, who is less to blame, has better chances of remarrying and to continue to be accepted in the community.

- The effect of court divorce is immediately valid and comes into force at the time of court decision which is documented and thus easily to prove in contrast to a private divorce, which is rarely made public. Another problem regarding the time when a private divorce is to take effect, is whether to depends on returning the dowry or not.[73]

5.2. Divorce Conditions and procedure

As previously mentioned, parties who want to divorce have to apply for this at an authorized court. The court, after considering the following, can adjudicate upon the divorce application.

- The first and most important reason for divorce is the failure of the marriage to achieve its basic objectives, which is, *inter alia*, procreation of children. Alternatives to divorce can be found, e.g. to marry a second wife without being divorced from the first one. Nevertheless, in such cases, as where the husband is impotent, divorce is unavoidable.[74]

- Another reason for divorce is irretrievable marriage breakdown. Even if husband and wife have children but, amicable living together has came to be impossible and every attempt and effort at a solution or mediation between them is unsuccessful, the only open door will be divorce. Reasons can be: Because of the wife's gross misconduct, repeated illness, ill treatment by the husband of his wife.

5.3. Legal Consequences of Divorce

Ending or dissolution of a marriage relation is followed by legal effects, which are related to matters like e.g. marital property, children and child custody and maintenance. Section 41 of the Re-statement of the Bahr el Ghazal Region Customary Law Act 1984 describes the legal effects to take place after poue-ruai divorce:

- Relieving the spouses of the obligation to continue their marital relationship,

- Freedom for the woman to marry another man, (and vice. versa).

- Recovery of the dowry cattle or property and offspring and all other rights due to the husband from his wife's relatives,

- Recovery of arueth(reverse payment) and all other rights due to the relatives of the divorced woman from the husband and his relatives,

- Right of the husband to take the children, if he pays aruok cattle to the relatives of his divorced wife.

Most conflict situations before the court are related to the cases of return of dowry and the right to take custody of the children.

Usually both matters are closely related to each other when a dispute about one of them arises. If the dispute cannot be settled between the parties, it needs to be referred to the court, which usually applies Dinka Law to the dispute.[75]

The main rule of Dinka Customary Law provides:

In the event of puoe- ruai, the husband and his kinsmen who contributed cows to the marriage, are entitled to recover the cattle they had paid as dowry. Equally, the bride's relatives are entitled to recover the arueth cattle they had paid to the husband and his kinsmen. The husband who has been just divorced or in case of his death the husband's father has the right to have custody of all the children of the marriage which has just been terminated.

The above- mentioned rule seems to mainly deal with returning the dowry and the right to take the children as a consequent effect, but there is another rule of Dinka customary law deals mainly with child custody, it provides:

The father of the children is entitled to custody when pouke- ruai lies in abeyance if he has not paid aruok cattle, which is five cows for each child or ten cows if the father failed or delayed to pay the aruok cattle to the children's maternal uncle before they became of age.

Section 10 of the Re-statement of the Bahr el Ghazal Region Customary Law Act 1984 describes, among others, the procedure to be followed in case of Aruok of children, it stipulates:

(..when divorce or dissolution of marriage takes place between a man and a woman, the relatives or the relative of the woman have the have the authority to retain the child or children into their custody If the father intends to have custody of his child or children, he shall pay to the woman or to the woman's relatives a specific number of cows for the child or each child. This payment of cattle for the redemption of a child or children by the father is called Aruok. There are some difficulties related to the exact interpretation and understanding of the wording which generally brings some practical problems with it. However, the legal practitioner must use each concept in a given situation to transmit a certain intention or to serve a certain purpose. All claims arising in connection with divorce e.g.. divorce related matters, should be settled in a Dinka court in a single suit, this procedure saves time and costs.

When a party to marriage submits a petition of divorce before a court and after hearing all available and related evidence, the court has to decide whether to permit divorce or not. If the court grants a divorce, then the procedure should move to the next step, which is to decide upon the returning of the dowry. The return of the dowry includes cattle provided as part of the dowry as well as of their offspring. If cattle comprising the dowry have been sold, have died or have become lost and negligence can be proved on the part of those due to return the dowry (the wife and her relatives), then the husband and his relatives are entitled to compensation. Another kind of claim that should be settled within divorce proceedings is related to aruok cattle.[76]

6. Divorce in Nuer Customary Law

Within the rules of divorce or dissolution of Nuer marriage, we have to distinguish between two main situations: dissolution of marriage on the death of the wife, and dissolution of marriage when both parties are still alive.

6.1 The Dissolution of Marriage on the Death of the Wife

Although the death of wife entitles her husband to dissolve the marriage and claim the return of his dowry, the enforcement of this right is very rare in the Nuer tribal community. It usually depends on many circumstances. It is unlikely to happen if the marriage relation lasted for a long time and children have arisen from it, especially not, if the husband besides this has had a good relationship with his wife's relatives.

There is a similarity to the above-mentioned *arouk* cattle situation, in the case of the Nuer. If children were born as a result of the marriage with the deceased wife, the father will, in any case, usually leave a sufficient number of cattle with his deceased wife's relatives to retain legal parenthood over children.[77]

The number of cattle left for this purpose varies from one group to another and also according to the sex of the children.[78]

In contrast to the situation with the Dinka, marriage among Nuer is possible for a dowry of less than fifteen head of cattle, and if some or all of them have perished or been lost (which was very frequent during the 1980's because of drought) no return of dowry should be claimed by the husband. although the right of the husband to a return of the dowry is undisputed, but, in fact disputes over the return of a dowry between a husband and relatives of his dead wife are in fact very rare. However, if the husband claims a return of the dowry, Nuer court will assert his right. If one child was born during the marriage, the kinsmen of the dead wife will return the dowry deducting a due number of cattle to compensate for the raising of the child. By an issue of two or more children arising from the marriage, usually there no return of dowry takes place.[79]

6.2 Divorce when both spouses are alive

This is the most common case for marriage dissolution proceedings before a Nuer court. The Nuer believe that there is no divorce without a reason: a Nuer court requires one or more of the following reasons to permit a divorce:

- The most common reason to claim a divorce is, if the wife is infertile in such a case, the husband can ask for a divorce and the return of the dowry. Not only for complete infertility but also even if wife gave birth to one or two children at the beginning of the marriage, but later, she was unable to give birth to more children - this can be regarded as a reason for divorce. In this case the dowry should be returned less the number of cattle required for legitimising the existing children.

- The breaking down of a normal relationship and a disharmonious day-to-day married life is a common reason for divorce not only in general but also amongst the Nuer. This is usually the case, when quarrels and nagging occur between husband and wife or between the wife and other wives, (if husband is married with two or more women) - also problems with the husband's relatives can lead to marital dissolution.

- Negligence of household duties by the wife is the third common reason for ending a marriage. A Nuer husband has a right to domestic and economic services from his wife, if she will fails to meet his expectations as to household order and duties, he can apply for a divorce.

- The committing of adultery by the wife is a further reason for the husband to file for divorce. However, usually it only comes to such a step if the wife will continue repeatedly to commit adultery.

- If a wife deserts her husband to live with another man, her husband is entitled to seek a divorce.

The above-mentioned reasons are the most common and well known for divorce amongst the Nuer. In most situations when the husband files for divorce, there is more than one reason e.g. the wife neglects her household duties and commits adultery and/or deserts her husband to live with. another man.

It worth mentioning, that this attitude of mind is not confined solely to the individual but extends to relatives, which means, despite having a good reason(s) for divorce, the plaintiff always needs to gain the support of relatives and the community.[80]

An aspect of inequality is to be seen when it is the wife who seeking a divorce. The reasons she has to provide her family with must be absolutely convincing compared by those of her husband. She has to convince her family that continuing marital life with her husband is impossible otherwise; the family may resists her demand to be divorced, taking into account, it is her family, which has to return the dowry. In spite of the difficulties facing a wife when seeking divorce, however, she may succeed, when one or more of the following reasons are valid:

- When her husband is impotent or infertile and thus unable to procreate children with his wife, then she can seek a dissolving of the marriage.

In such a situation, her family will usually support her in suing for a divorce, even if the family has to pay back a substantial dowry. Such a situation may occur when a family marries a daughter to an old man because of his wealth.

- If the husband is miserly and forbids his wife to make presents to family, relatives and neighbours, amongst the Nuer this is regarded as being a good reason to separate their daughter from such husband.

- When the husband fails to fulfil his economic duties or neglects to support his wife and children, the wife's family itself may seek dissolution of the marriage.

- Continual ill treatment or physical violence to the wife by her husband is a further reason for the wife and her family to request to dissolve the marriage.

Evidence of two or more of the above-mentioned reasons is usually a good enough ground for the wife's family to support her demand for a divorce. The wife's family in case of divorce may have to pay back a substantial dowry to the husband, but this be outweighed by other considerations. It is also her family's wish that she should has children and should have a happy married life with her husband. Her children, although legally in the patrilineal lineage of their father are also an asset to the maternal line.

Finally, it is the interaction of all these considerations and circumstances together which determines the stability of marriage or its need for dissolution. They are in fact features of the relations subsisting between the two families, starting with the relation between husband and wife, then through them to their own families and others relatives. [81]

Social and economical changes have also reached tribal communities like that of the Nuer and have influenced negatively the stability marriage and its long duration, which was previously believed to be a tradition rule.

These features are apparent not only in the increasing number of divorces but also in the growing body of law concerning marriage and divorce and in the number of registered judicial cases.[82]

7. Child Custody and Maintenance in Dinka Customary Law

Usually, regulation of matters like custody rights to children and disputes about maintenance arise after the divorce decision becomes final.

Dinka Customary rules regarding child custody share a main feature that marks all African customary rules concerning child welfare. Customary rules in Africa tend to give primacy to the maintenance of strong family ties over any other interests. However, in spite of the importance of these matters, there is no complete uniformity of legal rules within African communities. In other words as to the question of who should have the right of custody, and who has the obligations regarding maintenance and the question of the wife's maintenance - such issues may be brought before the court but also may not be. This can be explained by the fact that such issues often can be settled without court interference.

In general, according to Dinka customary law, as soon as the divorce has been announced, and the husband (who is the father of the children) met his obligation to provide *aruok* he is then authorized to keep or recover all children by him. If the divorced husband failed to provide arouk, the divorced wife (who is the mother of the children) and her relatives are entitled either to keep the children till the aruok- payment has been carried out or they keep part of the *thakha* for the children. Generally, there is no rule that provide that a child or children should remain with his/her their mothers until they reach a certain age.[83]

8. Regulation of Marital Property

One of the issues arising after a divorce has been decreed- "divorce-following-matters" is the distribution of marital property.

The regulation and distribution of property after divorce is relatively uncomplicated in the Dinka Community and in each tribal community in general compared with modern Western societies. This is related to the fact that property in tribal community is easy to "grasp". In large, modern communities, where both spouses possess significant property and are paid wages, related provisions, which regulate property and its distribution, are in consequence likely to be much more complicated.[84]

Where some statutory laws differentiate between property acquired before and during marriage, Dinka customary law regulates, dowry property, Arueth, Aruok-cattle all as marital property.

The most important moveable property consists of livestock that usually either belong to the husband or were acquired by him. Nevertheless, there are some cases, where livestock belongs to or has been acquired by the wife herself i.e. received as a gift or inherited before being married. In such cases, the wife is of course entitled to take it with her after divorce. She is also entitled to take domestic utensils and ornaments

In general, a wife is allowed to retain possession of her private property, that is property she brought with her at the time of marriage e.g. personal gifts made to her from her family, friends or others persons, items acquired through inheritance, gifts from her husband and from husband's family and also property acquired by the wife through her skill.[85]

There is a rule of Venda law in this regard that is worth mentioning because of its similarity to the Dinka rule "when spouses are divorced, the property in their household is to be divided accordingly to whether it is to stay or to be taken away by the respective owner. Everything belonging to the husband is put into his own category, no matter what class of goods or property it belongs to, because it remains his property in all circumstances. The wife has no claim to smallest part thereof. The wife's property (i.e. what is ordinarily considered hers when married) falls into four categories:

- What she was given by her husband and relatives,

- What she acquired by her own efforts, but belongs to her husband nevertheless,

- What she was given by her own relatives and,

- What she acquired by her own efforts and belongs to her entirely."

According to Dinka customary law, cattle, other livestock and movable property always belongs to the husband, unless the wife can provide proof of the opposite.

9. Child Custody and Maintenance in Nuer Customary Law.

If a marriage has been ended by divorce, the husband can claim legal parenthood of his children by providing a specific number of heads of cattle for the legitimization as legitimization fees to the family of his wife.

Fees payable for this purpose are different from one Nuer tribe to another and they call it *ruok gaanke* or *ruok muor*. According to some sources, the rate is five heads of cattle for a male child and six heads of cattle for a female child.[86]

Nuer Chiefs agree to higher fees for a female child than those for a male child because in the case of a girl the mother's family could expect to benefit materially on her marriage.

If marriage culminates in divorce or is dissolved because of the wife's death, personal items that are the property of the divorced wife go back to her (or to her family in the case of her death). All cattle should be returned to the husband with the above-mentioned deduction to retain legal parenthood of any children.[87]

When returning the dowry to the husband and his family, in theory, it must be the original dowry (and their offspring). However, in fact it is usually not possible to return the dowry exactly as received at the time of marriage. In such cases, where the original cattle have perished or got lost, a substitute must be returned, except in the following situations where no cattle are to be returned to the husband and his family:

- If the cattle perished due to disease or have been killed by wild animals or lost by reasons other than failure of responsibility or the negligence of the wife's family.

- If the cattle have been paid as compensation for homicide or in payment of fines imposed by the court.[88]

In all those cases, there will be no cattle return obligation on the part of the wife's family.

CHAPTER VI

CUSTOMARY RULES OF PROPERTY AND LEGAL OBLIGATIONS

1. Customary Dinka Rules regarding property

However, disputes regarding property rights in the Dinka community comprise the most important part of civil litigation, but Dinka language lacks legal terminology usually used in statutory legal systems to exactly describe such cases. Accordingly, for example, there is no exact expression that definitively stands for Law of Property alone, it can be described as „*long de kedè* but, on the other hand the word kedè means both property and thing. Especially the legal concepts related to property and the classification of it into movable and immovable property plays a minor role in Dinka Customary Law. In spite of the problem of finding appropriate legal terminology in the Dinka language that exactly corresponds with its equivalent in e.g. Common Law property matters and disputes has in Dinka Customary Law the same legal importance as it has in Common Law.

The procedure followed in Dinka Customary Law is to prove, whether an unlawful act violates a property right and in such cases to apply the appropriate remedy.[89]

1.1. Personal Property

Dinka customary rules regulating personal property have so far developed to cover the same legal sectors as recognised in Common Law. Nevertheless, they include general principles that regulate transfer of title to personal property: the rule is known as *Nemo dat quod non habet* which means: "No one can give a better title than his own; he can give possession, but not a title which is not vested in him".

A characteristic aspect of Dinka property rules is that transfer of property and the reclaiming of property are always mutually related.

The owner of property is entitled to reclaim his property from the hands of anyone who has acquired possession in good faith or bad faith from anyone who has no title to it.[90]

Only an owner can transfer his title. That means, it is the state of ownership not the possession that enables the transfer of a good title to another person. The legal owner will continue to maintain his title when the relevant object has been transferred illegally e.g. by theft, robbery or breach of trust.

On the other hand, the person illegally acquiring possession of the item in question has not the right to transfer the title to a third party. The third party acquiring possession of an illegally transferred item in good faith has to sue the second party to recover the payment.[91]

The same rule is applicable in case of knowingly acquired stolen property that may also lead to criminal procedure against the third party who has acquired the stolen property; furthermore, third party is not entitled to reclaim money paid for the property. It should be noticed that Dinka customary Property law gives more priority and weight to the civil procedure of the legal conflict, that is to say: the reinstatement of the legal ownership situation by returning title to the legal owner. The criminal procedure regarding illegally depriving an owner of his property and illegally transferring it to a third party are secondary.[92]

This leads to the conclusion, that the conviction of the person who committed theft or rubbery is not a pre-condition for the return of stolen property to its legal owner. There are no restrictions to the legal owner's right to transfer title to a third person.

If the borrower delivers a title as a debt security by lender, the legal ownership of title remains by borrower even if main debt has not yet been returned.[93]

That means the owner of property may transfer his legal title (right) to a third person even if it is burdened with debt.

The legal owner of property or title has the right to reclaim his property from a third person. e.g. if the transaction purpose, by which is meant the property that has been transferred does not exist for example if marriage is dissolved, the husband is allowed to pursue the dowry that is in the hands of his wife's relatives and claim for the return of it. This legal right is also asserted by section 53 of "The Restatement of the Baher el- Ghazal Region Customary Act 1984". When divorce or dissolution of marriage takes place, the husband is entitled to trace his cattle or property into the hands of anyone who has acquired possession or title to them from his in-laws through subsequent marriages, provided that he shall only be entitled to recover damages from his in-laws for any cattle or property delivered by them to the third parties through sale or discharge of certain obligations while the marriage was still valid".[94]

The right to claim recovery one's own property, although includes cattle's offspring, but does not extend to a compensation or a substitution of damaged property e.g. if the cattle which perished naturally while in the possession of the relatives or the transferee before the dissolution of the marriage.[95]

Furthermore gifts and donation received by a third party legally and in a good faith are not to be reclaimed by the original owner (first party) but the original owner however is entitled to claim compensation.

Section 61 of The Restatement of the Baher el- Ghazal Region Customary Act 1984 provides: "where a revocation of gift takes place, the donor (or the giver) is not entitled to trace the property given or donated into the hand of anyone who has lawfully or in good faith acquired possession or title to it before the revocation of gift is effected, but he is only entitled to recover damages from the donee or the receiver of the gift".[96]

The previously mentioned demonstrate cases, where a second party legally acquired and transferred property to a third party and the legal right of original owner to attempt to gain repossession.

However, section 57 of The Restatement of the Baher el- Ghazal Region Customary Act 1984 also covers cases of illegally acquisition of property by a third party. It allows the legal owner to pursue his property that has been acquired and kept by someone or transferred by this person to a third party.[97]

There are some exceptions as to the right of legal owner to attempt to reclaim his property that is in hand of other, those cases are:

- When it is impossible to recover the original property

If the property was lost or destroyed, in all such cases where the property does not exist anymore, compensation should be the only available remedy.

- When it is legally prohibited to make use of this right against some person or in some cases, e.g. when an innocent third party legally acquired the property in question from a second party when he was allowed to transfer or to pass it to third person.

However, in all these cases, the legal owner, despite locating the original property being either impossible or not allowed, then he is entitled to claim due compensation instead of his irrecoverable property.

1.2. Property obtained by Inheritance or Will

A person may also obtain property from a deceased relative as his legal successor or as testamentary regulated. If the deceased person did not leave a testament, then his estate goes to his wife or wives and children, and to his parents or instead to his brothers.[98]

The above-mentioned cases assume that successors to the family are alive. If this is not the case, the deceased's estate shall be transferred into the hands of a trustee.[99]

The trustee is then obliged to use part of deceased's property to marry for him. The deceased's new wife will then become the new trustee and is obliged to keep and administer the estate for the coming children, who will be regarded as the deceased's children and carry his name.

The regulation of inheritance property according to Dinka Customary Law has the following features:

- The deceased person or respectively the testator should has a family

- Property is the basic foundation for starting a family

- The deceased's property must remain within his family

- Property is regarded as being in family shared ownership

This family based ownership ideology of property in Dinka community leads to, among others, to restrictions regarding testamentary freedom. Although the testator is allowed to bequeath to a non-relative, the amount of this should not cover a major part of or all of the inheritance.

This can be explained by the fact that the property in question is not in the individual ownership of the testator but consists of contributions from all family members, not only living ones but also predecessors.

However, the trustee's main obligation is to form a family for the deceased person and his duties as such end with the transferring of the estate to the wife of the deceased, but his duties as supervisor over deceased's property continue until a male child of the wife of the deceased reaches the legal age of responsibility.

The parents of the deceased person will have to exercise parental care over the deceased's family. If they are too old or sick even to care for themselves, it is the duty of deceased's wife or wives and children to care for deceased's parents. Deceased's parents are also to share the estate's benefits with widow or widows and the children of their deceased son. If the deceased person has no own family, his brothers are obliged to take care of his estate and carry out the above-mentioned obligation of raising a family for the deceased.

Nevertheless, not all rights enjoyed by a deceased person are inheritable e.g. rights which also commonly enjoyed by other members of the community like fishing within tribal water or to graze livestock on tribal pasture.

1.3. The Land Property

Not only cattle form an important part of Dinka Customary Law of Property but also land property. Two laws regulate Land property in Sudan: the Settlement and Registration Act 1925 and the Unregistered Land Act 1970. Although the Settlement and Registration Act 1925 provides that all land, whether waste, forest, occupied or unoccupied falls within government property, customary rules have regulating power among tribal communities but are in accordance with the above-mentioned acts.

In general, the right of ownership to land is not exercised absolutely.

The rules of the Unregistered Land Act 1970 which was later repealed by the Civil Transaction Act 1984 seems to have application in rural areas Land may deemed to be subject to liabilities, rights, and interests even without registration or notification in the land register.

Although land property has the same importance within the Dinka community just like cattle property there is a principal philosophy that land is communal property. This explains why there are fewer conflicts concerning land compared with those regarding cattle. This has led to the fact that civil litigation regarding land are less frequent and this has contributed to the slow development of land law. Additionally commercial transactions regarding the transfer or disposal of land are rare. All of those factors contributed to place land property in second place behind cattle property.

Dinka differentiate between two types of land:

- The part of the high land on which domiciles are usually built and also partially used for farming is named b*aai* in the Dinka language.

The b*aai* land is high land, is suitable mainly for building homes, and is partially covered by forest. The usage of it is private or rather individual.

- The part of land, which should described as low land. It consists of the swamp area where lakes and rivers overflow their banks, it is known as *toc* in Dinka language. The *toc* has great economic importance for the Dinka. It is the grazing area for their cattle. The lakes and rivers are their fishing territorial. The swamp and costal areas used for planting after the flood return. The *toc* land is usually used as communal property of the tribal community.

The acquisition of land property is done by one of the method detailed below:

- Either by occupation: the ownership of unclaimed land can be acquired by occupation. This assumes that the occupier settles on the land with the intention of remaining on it and to use it continually.

- By conquest: this kind of land acquisition is only of historical important and belongs to past times, when the Dinka tribes were migrating from east to the west or to the areas where they are now domiciled.

- By way of gift and inheritance: a land property or a title to land can also be acquired by way of inheritance or as a gift.[100]

In general, the nature of the individual's right to land in the Dinka community as well as in other African communities, regarding the analyses of rights, claims, and liabilities is a complex one.

It is difficult to evaluate the exact nature of all those rights and claims especially because of the numerous economical, religious, political and social factors involved.[101]

The influence of religious and social factors is demonstrated in many cases. A claim to land can be asserted by such a fact as that the ancestors have died and are buried in the land in question, which establishes social connection to that land. The religious effect is illustrated in the belief, that the spirit of the "in this land buried ancestors" will help to them to remain there and to occupy the land. In spite of the wide acceptance of these beliefs among the Dinka tribes, there are some of them who recognize the loss of a private individual's right to arable land, which has been abandoned. Generally it be said, that the exclusive right of a man and his family to use the land and the inheritance of such land from generation to generation and the rights of the individual member of tribal community over the residential land even if such land has been abandoned, all point to the fact that the individual right in land may be seen as a right of ownership.[102]

The abovementioned is related to the individual's right to land. The ownership of an entire territory is held by the tribal community, inherited from first ancestors who settled on it as unoccupied land.[103]

However, despite vesting overall ownership rights in the tribal community, some authorities regard "indirectly" family's or individual's interest over arable land as a right of ownership.[104]

According to this opinion, that the individual's interest in residential and arable land is a right of ownership, leads to the assumption, that an individual may acquire the title to his residential and arable land in a manner, which is the same as the modes of acquisition of land by the community.

Another related matter concerns ownership of objects located on or in the land. The general rule is that things or objects located on or inside the land (attached to the land) belong to the owner of the land in question. Despite this general rule, a distinction must be drawn between particular objects. Animals and domestic animals are excepted from this rule since they have a legal owner. A land owner has property rights over things or objects "moveable or immovable" e.g. trees and their fruits to be found in his land.

Lost land title or property is usually seen in regard to individuals. It is thinkable that also a community may lose land property, but only if the entire tribal community migrates with the intention never to return, which rarely happens.

There are two opinions as to when an individual loses his ownership rights or his land title:

- According to the first opinion, a member of tribal community enjoys strong ties to his community as well as to his land located within this community residential area. These ties are so strong, that even if the individual abandoned it, it must be kept unoccupied unless he gives consent to a relative to take it over, and however, this opinion never claims that the individual would have an absolute right to the land.[105]

- The second opinion in this regard invokes a general rule. It confirms the loss of an individual's title or right to land as soon as he voluntarily abandons it and moves to settle elsewhere. The individual can always retain the title as long as his possession of the land in question is continuous.[106]

2. Customary Nuer Rules Regarding Property

Nuer use definite terms to describe ownership that are to be explained by the especial status of ownership relations within kinship.[107]

A Nuer person may speak of his cow *yang-da*" but also of his ownership or right to it. This right is qualified by his membership of a kinship group. Individual property or an individual's ownership of an object or thing in Nuer tribal community is mixed with kinship's ownership as to related object or thing. A Nuer person receives his property right from his relative(s), it is clear that it will not be his own indefinitely. He has to pass it further within the kinship group. This obligation is automatically attached to the received object or thing. In Nuer tribal community, cattle are part of a collective, not an individual system of ownership. A Nuer can rarely sell a cow without the express permission of his relatives.

Payment of dowry in form of cattle in this regard is not a financial transaction but an operation that maintains the balance of exogamous groups, defines their limits, and emphasizes the legality of the marriage.

The same is valid for land ownership. There is no concept of ownership of land by the individual. Ownership of the land, whether for cultivation or for grazing as well as fishing area is expressed as collective ownership by the kinship group. Ownership in this sense follows the lines of social cleavage. Disputes over land are again associated with the balanced opposition of tribal segments, not of individuals.

Apart from cattle and land there are other forms of property, e. g. clothes, household articles, weapons and tools, the ownership of which is in some cases more individual in character.

The descendants of the original occupiers of the land usually hold rights in land as well as in pasture and fishing. This description fits especially for Eastern Nile Nuer. Their ancestors seized the area from the Dinka about the end of the nineteenth century.

Occupation of the land and respective rights to a certain territory are often expressed in mythological terms linked to the history of the original lineage. The original ancestor is said to have divided land among his sons, themselves ancestors of particular collateral lineages, in the same way as he divided his cattle and ritual functions among them. Nevertheless, this is merely an idiom, which gives emotional emphasis to ownership of land vested in that original lineage, for land, either arable or pasture, is not a form of property that is normally controlled by the laws of inheritance. The eldest son will inherit hut(s) and cattle byres, while the other sons continue to occupy them so long as they wish to do so, especially if they are not married. The youngest sons do not have specific portions of their father's land, and there is consequently no individual inheritance of land. [108]

Land ownership among Nuer includes three types of land. When a Nuer speaks of his *rol* by which he means his country or sometimes his *dhor* he means a territory, which includes the high land used for cultivations and permanent settlements, middle land for pasture and water- covered land used for fishing and for watering cattle.

Territory and rights in land follow a segmentary system. However, individuals or even small groups of people need not confine their movements to the territory of the segment to which by tradition and practice they should belong.[109]

From a legal point of view, generally there are rarely complicated disputes among Nuer, whether between individuals or collective groups, regarding rights in arable land.

During the cultivation season the Nuer occupy the high ground which is free from river floods or swamping by heavy rain. The high land is limited in area when compared to the total area occupied by Nuer tribes, but there is generally more than enough available. This in spite of the fact that the Nuer do not use fences or similar boundaries to separate and limit their land from a neighbouring one. A widely structured and complex set of legal rules regulating land property among Nuer is not necessary and will not be needed unless there is a shortage of land which in not usually the case.[110]

3. Dinka Customary Rules of Obligations

Dinka Customary Law includes rules regulate duties as well as liabilities based on law of obligations. Such duties and liabilities have a tortious original imposed by law and owed to the public or of contractual nature towards a particular person or group. In the following are the details of each.

3.1. Obligations Based on Contract

One of the widely- known contractual transaction in Dinka commercial community is debt security know as *Amuk* or *Amec*. Section 64(a) of the Restatement of the Baher el Ghazal Customary Act 1984 describes it as: any property delivered by a debtor named *raan-koony* to a creditor named *raan kony* as a form of security or guarantee for the repayment of a debt known as *keny* or discharge of an existing obligation also called *keny*.

According to s. 64(b) if the debtor fails completely to repay the debt at the time fixed or at the period which the Court may consider to be reasonable in the circumstances where no fixed period for the discharge of the debt was agreed upon at the time of the contract, the secured creditor is entitled to take over the property he possesses as 'amuk'. While the creditor obtains the legal possession, the debtor continues to keep ownership. The creditor is obliged to exercise reasonable care for the safety of the debt- security in his possession.[111]

Although the creditor according to the above-mentioned section has the legal position of a trustee of property, however the degree of care he has to exercise is higher. Another feature is the contractual feature of the relationship between the two parties, which impose mutual obligations on both and differentiates it from trust.[112]

The majority of litigation cases are related to disputes over amuk. although the law provides clear regulations in this regard, parties usually face a conflict that necessitates court involvement to be resolved, especially when the parties fail to state a date to repay the debt and refund security or when the creditor maliciously keeps or transfers amuk.[113]

3.2. Obligations based on Tortious Liability

A person is obliged to compensate another person for damages, either if he caused it himself or if caused by his animals.

Liability for damages caused by domestic animals is classified in Dinka customary law according to the category animal belong to.

Dinka divide domestic animals into two categories:

- Animals of recognized social and economical value e.g. cattle, goats and sheep.

- Domestic animals with less, or without social or economic, value e.g. horses, donkeys, dogs or cats.

The importance of animal is the basis of liability.

The person in charge of an animal (owner) is liable for the damage or damages caused by this in one of three cases:

- Where the animal causes damage to the property of another person. The person in charge is obliged to compensate the person whose property was damaged in accordance with section 79 of the Dinka Customary Law Act 1984.[114]

- When the animal causes or inflicts injury to another person. In such a case, the liability of the person in charge of the animal or of the keeper depends upon whether the injured is a trespasser or not and whether the injury inflicted by an animal belongs to the first or second category. Usually, if the injured person is legally at the place where the injury inflicted upon him/her and the injury caused by an animal is of the first category, there is no compensation due.[115]

- When the animal causes death or injury to another animal. A compensation is only due if the act fulfilled the following conditions: (1) the animal has been injured or killed within the premises of its owner or keeper, (2) the animal causing injury or death must have entered the premises as a trespasser. The owner or person in charge of the animal (that caused injury or death) is obliged to compensate the person who suffered the loss of his animal according to section 80 of Dinka Customary Law Act. 1984.[116]

CHAPTER VII

CUSTOMARY CRIMINAL LAW

The classification of topics within this chapter under the heading criminal law is only a matter of simplifying the study by categorizing it, as jurists usually know it.

It must be emphasized again, that neither Dinka customary law nor Nuer customary law know the division of customary rules according to their nature into civil and criminal rules. This explains why offences usually categorized as falling under criminal law studies in statutory laws, but those customary laws to be found among rules of civil nature

Not only is the classification of offences under civil rules a feature of customary law but also the nature of related punishments. Punishments for homicide and adultery have the character of compensation due as remedies for breach of contractual or tortious obligations under civil law.

1. Classification and Regulation of Homicide and Bodily Injuries in Dinka Customary Law

Besides the above-mentioned explanation for the classification of homicide and related offences under civil matters, there is an additional aspect: It is the fact that even a criminal act also includes a feature that qualifies it as a tort. A criminal act against a person or persons causes some loss for which due remedy is material or financial compensation. This is a characteristic of Dinka Customary Law, which not concerned with punishment but in restoration of the social equilibrium through the payment of compensation. The compensation paid in a case of homicide is known as *apuk* in the Dinka language, it is always paid in cattle i.e. 30 cows for a person.

Some researchers believe that the payment of cattle compensation has the objective of providing enough dowry for the deceased's family so that they can procure a wife for the deceased.[117]

A further feature that distinguishes Dinka Customary Law from State Law is collective responsibility. The person who committed homicide stands not alone with the liability to pay compensation, his family and relative as well carry this responsibility along with him and they are obliged collectively to contribute to the gathering and payment of the requested compensation. Such collective responsibility in the above-mentioned sense comes into force only in cases of homicide and serious bodily injuries. The collective nature of liability for compensation crosses the border (of the murderer and his family) to include the whole tribe, when a person or persons were killed in fight between two or more tribes and the killer is unknown. The tribe to which the (unknown) person responsible for the death belongs to has to pay collectively the apuk due.[118]

It is important to mention that such elements, which usually in state law may have an effect on the definition of the criminal act or play a great role in determining due punishment, such elements usually remain regardless in Dinka Customary Law concerning applicable rule for homicide and related compensation.[119]

This is because of the previously mentioned main objective of Dinka Customary Law in restoring of the social equilibrium (the status quo) and maintenance of peace.[120]

However, there are a few exceptions to the previously mentioned general rule. There are two cases, where the killer's state of mind plays a role in decreasing the compensation payable. These cases are:

- The case of incapacity and mental disability, this includes such cases, where the accused suffers mental disability, insanity or minor, the reduced or diminished liability affects the payable amount of apuk (compensation) and reduces the number of cattle payable to ten.[121]

- The case of accidental killing, the same to be followed in cases where the act leading to death accidentally inflicted.[122]

Even in cases where death is caused intentionally by a relative, the accused and his agnatic relatives are obliged to pay compensation in full. If the act leading to death was unintentional, no apuk needs be paid, except for a small number of cattle to be used to appease the soul of the deceased person.[123]

Where a married woman intentionally causes the death of her husband, it is her own family that has to pay apuk to her husband's family.[124]

If she intentionally causes the death of a person other than her husband or a relative, her husband and his relatives are obliged to pay the apuk.[125]

A husband who intentionally causes the death of his wife is also, together with his relatives responsible. The marriage is automatically dissolved in both cases of killing either by the wife or husband. In the latter case, the wife's relatives are allowed to keep the dowry instead of receiving apuk.[126]

2. Homicide and related offences in Nuer Customary Law

The Nuer are "hot-blooded", fighting between members of the same community or against other tribes is not a rare incident. The attitude of hostility often spreads to a much larger group. Fighting usually ranges from a minor clash between a few individuals within the group, community or tribe to major clashes with neighbouring tribes. Fighting is sometimes described as the national pastime of the Nuer, however, is not so much a pastime as a necessary means of protecting individual and collective rights in the absence of an established authority by which rights can be maintained. This was the situation after establishing the Chiefs' Courts.

However, cases of self-justice are going back, self-justice and retaliations are still existing in the Nuer tribal community.[127]

The Nuer already agree to the fact that homicide is wrong, they call it *"duer"*, fighting is undesirable and means a threat to peace. It must be considered, that homicide among Nuer usually leads to countless blood feuds. Such blood feuds are characteristic of the relations prevailing between the political divisions of a tribe. The Nuer, like many other tribal communities, believe that the relative's ties demand acts of revenge against the killer of a family or community member.

There was no conception of individual punishment to be inflicted on the person of the killer in the time prior to Chiefs' Courts Ordinance.

The Nuer tribal community place great emphasis on the necessity and importance of restoring social equilibrium. However a settlement is in no sense an individual affair; it is not necessary to take revenge on the person of the killer himself; any one of his family or relatives would do instead. Killing a person of the other family, group or tribe is seen as restoring the balance by reducing their numbers in the same way.

On the other side, the Nuer acknowledge, that the principle of a life for a life, although it satisfies honour needs for a while, does not lead to permanent peace. Restoration of social equilibrium requires positive action to restore peace and avoid continuing blood feuds. A positive settlement by payment of compensation is the favoured solution.

However, settlement by payment of compensation depends largely on the degree of social integration and independence of the groups involved. These situations belong now to the past, after the establishing of Chiefs' Courts and the enactment of the related Ordinance, homicide has became a criminal offence and strong action is taken to prevent the continuation of a feud.

Homicide is legally punished, but the feud is still traditionally widespread even if compensation has already been paid. The payment of compensation in cattle is still made as a positive and effective way of restoring the balance and allowing social and economic contacts to continue. The deceased must be married to a wife so that his "life" continues in children carrying his name.[128]

This is why that the compensation has to have a relation to the dowry and should theoretically be in proportion to current rates of dowry, however, the proportion is not exact since there are other claims that have to be met.[129]

The killer is not allowed to eat, drink or shave his head and his home remains closed until a "Leopard-Skin" has let his blood.[130]

The traditional number of cattle due as compensation for homicide amongst the Nuer is forty head. A small number of Nuer tribes demand fifty head for pre-meditated murder; this is the case when e.g. the murderer used a fighting-spear as the deadly weapon.[131]

Full compensation is payable even if the injured person dies a year later from his wounds - this is still regarded as a normal murder.

The compensation for accidental killing usually paid on a reduced scale. The accidental killing of a relative is a minor wrong amongst the Nuer, which will demand only token compensation and ritual expiation.[132]

A Nuer man, who seduces an unmarried girl, who dies as a result of this when giving birth to the child, is obliged to pay her relatives compensation. Killing in a fair fight is also seen as offence against Nuer standards of chivalry and results in compensation, which however less than that due when killing a person by stealth or ambush.

The above-mentioned is not applied when the person killed does not belong to a Nuer tribe, i.e. a Dinka person, who has no connexion with Nuer and does not live among them. The value of compensation varies according to the tribe. Also for killing of a person believed to posses the evil eye "peth" only a reduced compensation of six heads of cattle to be paid to his relatives.[133]

Although Nuer do not normally intentionally kill women, however in cases, where this may have happened, full compensation is to be paid. There is no distinction relating to compensation payable based on gender

Compensation for killing a married woman is to by paid to her husband. Part of the compensation must be paid to her family, if her husband paid only part of the dowry.

A husband is responsible in the same way as with the Dinka for his wife's actions if she is legally married, i.e. if she kills someone, then it is her husband, who has to pay due compensation, not her family.[134]

Injuries, others than those causing immediate death, also result in the need for cattle compensation in different scales according to Nuer Customary Law. The compensation is intended not only to calm the feelings of the injured person, but also to restore the social balance between the conflicting parties.

There are many injuries recognized as due to be compensated in Nuer Customary Law i.e. for an injury resulting in permanent disability six heads are due, the loss of one eye, five heads, for the fracture of the forearm two heads.[135]

3. Adultery in Dinka Customary Law

Just like homicide, adultery, which is known as "*Akor*" in the Dinka language is usually seen as an offence, however, in Dinka Customary Law it is regulated under civil matters. Adultery as illegal sexual intercourse between a man and married woman is recognized as a grave offence against marriage in all African legal systems, but also as a civil wrong.[136]

Dinka Customary Law includes sanctions against adultery, which are of a legal as well as of religious nature.

The general rule is that, every Dinka woman, who is not a girl, is presumed to be a married woman. The liability of any man who commits sexual intercourse with her is strict one.[137]

In others words, it is the responsibility of the adulterer to make sure that the woman, with whom he has sexual intercourse is not a married woman. The compensation to be paid by the adulterer (six cows and one bull) is such a major deterrent that rarely would a Dinka man risk losing so much for a transient form of enjoyment.[138]

If a married woman commits adultery twice or more, her husband or his successor is not allowed to claim compensation for the adultery committed, if compensation for first adultery has been fully paid. The second adulterer as well as any further adulterers who have committed adultery with same woman will be punished with imprisonment, a fine, or both.[139]

A relative of the husband, who commits adultery with this wife shall pay one cow as compensation, if he contributed to the dowry paid by the husband, otherwise he is obliged to pay the full compensation.[140]

The right to sue an adulterer and claim compensation is held by the husband, if the husband is dead, it is his successor who can make use of it.[141]

A husband who has filed for divorce or dissolution of marriage because of adultery, has the right to claim and receive compensation before the divorce shall take place.[142]

If a child or children are conceived as the result of an adulterous union, they carry the name of the husband and are regarded as marital children unless the husband has sued for divorce. In the case of divorce or dissolution of marriage because of adultery, the child or children resulting from the illegal sexual intercourse between the wife and other man belong(s) then to the wife's family.[143]

When a woman who has committed adultery with another man is divorced after the 'akor' cattle have been obtained by the husband, the title to the cattle shall pass to her relatives, provided that the Court may allow the husband to retain them by way of a set-off when he is exerting a claim for the recovery of the dowry cattle or property from her relatives.[144]

4. Adultery in Nuer Customary Law

Nuer courts do not start procedure unprompted, a party or the parties to a conflict must refer the dispute to the court so that the legal proceedings start to operate. This is unless a "criminal" law has been broken and a criminal offence has taken place. Disputes regarding marriage and related matters like the distribution of a dowry are rarely brought to court.

Nevertheless, it is not only the problem in defining adultery which make it difficult for courts to intervene, there are also many other factors. The Nuer do not place great importance on physical paternity. Often an old Nuer man or an impotent one may seek the help of another man to have sexual intercourse with his wife, so that she bears children that will inherit his name and property.

In spite of the above-mentioned facts and the relaxed attitude to physical paternity within the Nuer community, adultery is still seen as wrongdoing and violates the husband's rights regarding his wife. It requires compensation in the form of cattle. The compensation claim will nearly always to be enforced by a court unless certain circumstances are considered to mitigate the offence. The compensation for adultery, almost among all Nuer tribes, consists of six heads of cattle. The first five of the cows are direct compensation to the husband for the injury inflicted upon his marriage relationship and the sixth one is for ritual purposes.

It is unclear, why the husband has to return the compensation in case of a childbirth resulting from the adultery that took place between his wife and another man.[145]

In Deng Kac v. Nyuon Makwac: Nyuon Makwac committed adultery with the wife of Deng Kac. He admitted his guilt before the court, and was therefore sentenced to pay six head of cattle. But he paid only three head of cattle, before paying the rest eighteen months later. He appealed against the court decision because Deng's wife had in the interim born a child. Nyuon did not only claim the right to hold back the rest of the cattle due, he furthermore claimed for the return of two of the already delivered cows one to be kept by as yang kule.[146].

Nuer law, in opposition to that of the Dinka, allows compensation claims for adultery by a husband for the same wife once, but no more than twice.

Compensation is also payable in the case of a widow who commits adultery without the permission of her husband's legal successor.

However, the successor or the legal trustee of the deceased husband rarely make use of this right. It usually depends upon many elements, among others e.g. the age of the woman and her relation to her husband's family, also whether the man with whom she committed adultery is a relative or not.[147]

In a specific case, Jegh (male) married Nyabwogh (female), Jegh died shortly after the wedding.

Tec, who was one of Jegh's heirs was unmarried, he wanted to live with Jegh's widow "Nyabwogh". Nyabwogh preferred however to stay with another man named Kwoiny Ruok instead. Tec made many efforts to persuade her to return to him, but she refused. He then went to court and judgment was given that Kwoiny, who was deemed responsible for enticing Nyabwogh away, should pay one cow as yang kule to Tec. His act was considered to be adultery. The court ordered the immediate return of Nyabwogh to Tec.[148]

The same general rule mentioned previously is applicable for a "Ghost-wife" who is actually married to the deceased's heir but legally she is the deceased's wife. In a case of adultery, the heir is entitled to claim compensation as mentioned in Tec Nyagh v. Kwoiny Ruok. By adultery with a relative of husband the full rate of compensation is usually demanded unless the husband and the have a close relationship.

Final Notes

Finally, taking into consideration the arguments explained in the foregoing chapters and bearing in mind the importance of customary rules in a tribally structured society such as Sudanese society, especially in Southern Sudan. One has no other choice but to admit the necessity and importance of respecting ethnic identity and diversity, especially that of those non-Arabic Sudanese communities and tribes. Respecting ethnic diversity and the recognition of tradition seem to be one of the significant factors needed to enable equal right for all Sudanese and to give value to the possession of a Sudanese identity.

The way to achieve this objective must be paved by laws and rules as chosen and thus accepted by the concerned Sudanese community in each region. Politicians must stop pursuing their own interests. Bribery, corruption, racial and ethnic hatred, preferring and benefiting one's own relatives (nepotism) and similar egoistic types of behaviour needs to be greatly reduced or eliminated. The Sudanese people have suffered not only with the coming of the first military dictatorship, but also during short-lived civil governments that have proved to be more corrupt and less competent to govern the country than the military.

The future of the Sudan does not lie in trying to arabize or Islamise its people by all possible means. The future of Sudan depends on recognition of its ethnic diversity and by it fairly sharing the produce and riches of its soil. Having the same rights for all Sudanese, whether from East, North, South or West Sudan is the first and essential step for staring a democratic national dialogue by which all Sudanese can plan their future together, regain the feeling of being equal citizens and bear together the responsibility for dealing with what may face them in the future.

The forgetting of these essential principles of a secure democracy caused the outbreak of the first civil war in southern Sudan, but it is the ignorance of this fact, which has led to a second outbreak of a civil war that lasted for more than thirty years. As if it was not enough learn from bloodily written initial lesson. The same mistakes lay behind the emerging conflicts in the Nuba Mountains and later in Eastern Sudan and in the Dar Fur region. When will the Sudanese draw their lessons from these conflicts, and what is necessary to make them recognise what needs to be done – and then act on it?

APPENDIX

THE RE-STATEMENT OF BAHR EL GHAZAL REGION CUSTOMARY LAW (AMENDED) ACT 1984 BAHR EL-GHAZ-AL REGION ACT NO. 1, 1984

In accordance with the provisions of Section 55, 57 of the Presidential Order No. 1, 1983 and Regulation 35(1) of the People's Regional Assembly, Conduct of Business Regulations, 1983, the People's Regional Assembly, Bahr El-Ghazal Region, hereby pass the following amended Act:

PART 1
CHAPTER 1

Section 1
Title and Commencement

This amended Act shall be called the Re-Statement of Bahr El -Ghazal Region Customary Law (Amended) Act 1984, and shall come into Operation as an Act, on the date of its signature by the Governor of the Region.

Section 2
Repeal

The Bahr El -Ghazal Province Local Order No. 1 of 18th of December 1975 is repealed.

Section 3
The Law to apply in certain cases

(i) Whenever a conflict arises between any Customary Law embodied in this amended Act and the provisions of the general territorial State Law, the State Law shall prevail.

(ii) Whenever a Court does not find an appropriate customary rule applicable to a case before it, in this Act, recourse shall be made to any appropriate Customary Rule in existence.

Section 4
Penalty, Damages or Compensation

(i) Damages or compensation awarded under this amended Act shall not prevent the Court from imposing any other penalty authorized by law, provided damages or compensation recoverable shall be taken into account in assessing the other penalty.

(ii) Where the award is in cattle, goats, spears and so forth, the Court making the order for payment, or the Court executing it, or the parties themselves, may assess current market value of the property awarded and proceed to execute payment in money or in any other property.

Section 5
Court

"Court" means the Local Courts and State Courts.

PART 2
CHAPTER 2
THE CODE OF DINKA CUSTOMARY LAW

Section 6
Title

This law shall be called the Code of the Dinka Customary Law.

Section 7
Application

The provisions of this Regional Code shall apply throughout the Region of Bahr EI-Ghazal to the following types of persons and situations:

(a) All Dinka of Bahr El-Ghazal Regions.

(b) All persons involved in sexual offences or acts with Dinka girls, wives or women of Bahr El -Ghazal Regions.

(c) All persons who have adopted the Dinka way of life or have accepted to be bound by Dinka Customary Law as practiced in this Region.

(d) Personal disputes connected with marriages, divorce, custody of children and their redemption, provided the woman in respect of whom such claims arise comes from a family subject to the Dinka Customary Law as applied in Bahr El-Ghazal Region.

(e) Tortious acts committed within this Region against a Dinka of Bahr El-Ghazal Region by non-Dinka or Dinka outside the Region, provided that such actors are subject to customs similar to those of the Dinka in the field of compensation, or homicide and personal injuries, provided also that such acts are not already regulated by some border Agreements.

(f) Gifts and intestate or testate succession where the donor or the deceased is subject to the Dinka Customary Law of this Region.

GENERAL EXPLANATIONS AND DEFINITION

Section 8
Bridewealth Hock- thiek

The term "*hok- thiek*" means the cattle payable by a bridegroom or husband and his Kinsman to the Kinsman of the bride or wife as consideration for the marriage.

Section 9
Arueth

"*Arueth*" means the property or cattle payable to the husband and his Kinsman, in a certain proportion to the bridewealth cattle or property, after the conclusion of marriage.

Section 10
Aruok of Children

When a girl or an unmarried woman has been pregnant without being married by the man who has impregnated her, or when divorce or dissolution of marriage takes place between a man and a woman, the Kinsman of the impregnated girl or unmarried woman, or the woman whose marriage has been dissolved, have the power to retain the child or children into their custody. If the father intends to obtain his child or children, he shall pay to the girl's or woman's Kinsman a specific amount of cows for the child or each child. This payment of cattle for the redemption of a child or children by the father is called Aruok'.

Section 11
Adultery "Akor"

(a) The word 'Akor' means adultery with a married woman. It further means cattle or property payable as damages by the man who commits adultery with a married woman, to the husband or his successor or agent or trustee.

(b) 'Akor', in the sense of adultery, means commission of sexual intercourse between a married woman and another man without the husband's consent.

Section 12
Awac

(i) The word 'Awac' literally means a mistake or offence. It also means cattle or property payable to a party aggrieved by the breach of marriage relations, or damages payable by a person who impregnates rapes or elopes with a girl or woman or any party whose reputation has been injured by the publication of a defamatory material. "Awac" has a penal feature.

Awec

(ii) It means a payment for conciliation or an appeasement. It is civil in nature.

Section 13
Tiop

It means the amount of cattle payable by a man whose wife is dead to her relatives when the marriage is treated as dissolved by such death.

Section 14
Incest "Akeeth"

Akeeth means the commission of sexual intercourse between a man and a woman who have blood relationship either from the paternal or maternal side. Sexual intercourse of this nature is believed to affect the health of the woman afterwards and the health of the children she will produce, unless some religious purification is undertaken after she has confessed the identity of all the Relatives who have had sexual intercourse with her.

Section 15
Relative

The word 'relative' in this Code (Act, Part II) includes parents, brothers and sisters, guardians, maternal uncles and paternal uncles who are bound, when there is marriage, to contribute some cattle towards the bridewealth, or contribute by paying some cattle for apuk when another person is killed, or who are entitled to share in bridewealth property when a girl is married or share in apuk cattle, when a person of one blood has been killed by another person.

Section 16
Parents and stepbrothers

'Parents includes 'stepfathers and brothers includes 'step-brothers'.

Section 17
Apuk

'Apuk'means the act of paying cattle or other property as damages by the accused or the accused and his relatives to the relatives of the person whom he has killed or the person whom he has injured.

Section 18
Werpiu or Lok- thok

(a) When a Dinka man marries, he is bound by a customary rule to abstain from eating any food or drinking anything that belongs to or which has been prepared by his in-laws. After the conclusion of such marriage, his in-laws must give him a heifer. When he receives the heifer, the elders among his in-laws carry out a religious ceremony by sprinkling him with water. This process of sprinkling with water before he can drink or ear from his in-laws is called 'Werpiu' or 'Lok-thok'. The heifer which is given to him by his in-laws for this purpose is called Dan-werpiu'or 'Lok-thok'.

(b) For the purpose of this law, a person or an animal dies naturally or a thing or property is destroyed or damaged naturally when he/it is not killed or damaged or destroyed by a human being.

CHAPTER 3
PERSONAL LAW

Section 19
Definition of Ruai marriage

Subject to other provisions of this Law, a Dinka ruai or marriage is a Union between one man, or his successor, or his trustee and one or more women for their lives for the purpose of sexual cohabitation, procreation of the young and maintenance of the homestead, provided that such a union may take place between one barren or childless woman and another for whom male consorts are provided; provided also that such a Union may take place between a deceased male and one or more women through his successor or trustee.

Section 20
Consent Game- ruai

(a) The only consent, which is material for the conclusion of a valid ruai or marriage, is that of the parents, brothers and those paternal uncles of the spouses.

(b) When a man and a woman have taken each other as husband and wife without the consent of their relatives, such a union may be dissolved or confirmed by such relatives.

Section 21
Capacity "Dit"

(a) No marriage shall be consummated between a boy and a girl until both of them have attained maturity.

(b) Determination of maturity: For a gin, the beginning of maturity age is marked by the first period of menstruation, while for the boy, it is marked by certain physical or biological changes, such as vocal change, growth of hair in the arm-pits or by or by traditional marks designed to mark the end of the period of boyhood.

Section 22
Bridewealth "Hok- thiek"

The Relatives of both parties to a marriage shall be free to fix the amount of cattle or amount of property payable as 'Hok-thiek' bridewealth. They shall also be free to fix the manner and time of delivery of such cattle or payment of such property.

Section 23
Form of marriage

(a) A formal marriage is established by undertaking the procedure of (i) engagement (thuot), (ii) agreement (luele-ruai) and (iii) ceremony accompanying the delivery (atoc) of the bnde (apuoc-thiaak) to her bridegroom (ame-thiek).

(b) Failure to follow the stages mentioned in (a) above except (ii) does not affect the marriage validity.

Explanation: The agreement referred to in (a) (ii) above refers to the agreement between the Relatives of the spouses.

Section 24
When the Court fixes the amount of bridewealth cattle

When a man takes a woman as his wife but neglects or refuses or otherwise fails to pay any bridewealth cattle on property to her Relatives, or when the whole marriage is in dispute, the Court may enforce the marriage. When the Court enforces the marriage, it shall order the man, together with his Relatives to pay thirty cows and six bulls as bridewealth (Hok-thiek), provided that the Court shall always have the power to over-ride the will of the Relatives of both spouses.

Section 25
The following rights accrue from the outset of the marriage to the husband and Relatives.

(i) Delivery of the bride to the bridegroom by her Relatives.

(ii) Payment of 'Arueth' cattle by the bride's Relatives to the husband and his Relatives.

(iii) Payment of a heifer (or a cow) for 'werpiu' or 'lok-thok' to the bridegroom.

(iv) Payment of a heifer for 'Wan'or 'Ahoth' to the bride-groom.

(v) Claim of a share in the bridewealth of the bridegroom's younger Sister-in-law or sisters-in-laws who is or arc subsequently married.

Section 26
Rights accruing to the family of the bride

Payment of the bridewealth or property to them by the Relatives of the bridegroom.

Section 27
Adultery "Akor"

Presumption of marriage: Any Dinka who is not a girl is presumed to be a married woman and any man who commits sexual intercourse with such a woman does so at his own risk.

Section 28
Number of cattle "Akor cattle"

When a man commits adultery with a married woman, he shall pay six cows and one bull to the husband or his successor as 'akor' or 'aruok' and no penalty may be passed against hirn by the Local Court, but if he has no cattle to pay as 'akor', he shall be punished with irnprisonment or fine or with both as prescribed by the Sudan Penal Code.

Section 29
No payment of 'Akor' cattle, if adultery is committed for a second time.

When a married woman commits adultery for a second time with another man after the 'akor' cattle have been paid for the first act of adultery, the husband or his successor or trustee is not entitled to claim any 'akor' cattle again, but the man who commits the offence shall be punished with imprisonment or fine or both in accordance with the provisions of the Sudan Penal Code.

Section 30
The party to sue in adultery cases

The husband, or if he is dead, his successor is the only competent party to sue in the case of adultery.

Section 31
Adultery committed by a married woman with the husband's relative.

Whenever a woman commits adultery with a relative of her husband who has contributed a cow or some cows during her marriage as part of the bridewealth, the relative who commits the offence is only bound to pay a cow to the husband or his successor or trustee as 'awec', but if such relative never paid any cow or some cows as his contribution to the bndewealth, he is bound to pay six (6) cows and one bull as 'akor' (or 'aruok') to the husband or his successor.

Section 32
Child who is the product of adultery

The child who is the product of a sexual intercourse between a married woman and another man belongs to the legal father. But, if the legal father elects to divorce his wife and disowns the child, his wife's Relatives will be entitled to have the child.

When a husband is compellable to sue for 'Akor' cattle

When a man whose wife has committed adultery with another person elects to divorce her, he is bound or compelled by the Court to sue the offender in order to obtain 'akor' cattle before the divorce or the dissolution of the marriage is granted.

Section 33
When a husband is compellable to use for "Akor" cattle

When a man whose wife has committed adultery with another person elects to divorce her, he is bound to or compelled by the Court to sue the offender in order to obtain "akor" catlle before the divorce or the dissolution of the marriage is granted.

Section 34
Passing of the title to adultery cattle where divorce takes place

When a woman who has committed adultery with another man is divorced after the 'akor' cattle have been obtained by the husband, the tide to the cattle shall pass to her Relatives, provided that the Court may allow the husband to retain them by way of a set-off where he is exerting a claim for the recovery of the bridewealth cattle or property from her Relatives.

Section 35
Divorce "Puoki- ruäi"

A valid divorce shall always be granted by the Court with the consent of all or more interested parties to the marriage contract.

Section 36
Grounds for granting divorce "Puok- ruäi"

A Court may grant divorce, if requested, on any one of the following grounds:

(1) Barrenness of the wife.

(2) Impotence of the husband.

(3) Death of all or more children of the spouses.

(4) Akeeth (Incest).

(5) Woman's gross misconduct.

(6) Cruelty to the wife by her husband or his Relatives.

(7) Infectious or venereal disease passed on to the complaining spouse by the other.

(8) Deterioration of relations between the Relatives of the spouses.

Section 37
When a Count may refuse to grant 'puok divorce"

A Court may refuse to grant divorce, if it is of the opinion that the marriage relationship has been established for a long period or on account of the amount of children born during the Union of the spouses.

Section 38
When death may terminate marriage relations

Death of the wife may terminate the marriage relations between the spouses, but the death of the husband has no such effect.

Section 39
Parties to divorce suit

The following parties may sue for divorce before the Court:

(1) The husband or his successor or consort or trustee.

(2) The wife or her parents or guardian, provided that the Court seeks before it, the attendance of all or more parties who are bound by the marriage contract to give their consent to the divorce.

Section 40
Valid divorce or dissolution of marriage to take place in Court

No valid divorce or dissolution of marriage relationship shall take place outside the Court through:

(1) Mutual agreement of the Relatives of the spouses.

(2) Mutual agreement of the spouses.

(3) Unilateral decision of any one of the spouses, but if the parties have adopted outside the Court any of the above methods, the Court shall not lend its aid or authority to any one of the parties who fails to obtain his or her rights against the other party thereafter.

Section 41
Effects of the dissolution of marriage or divorce puok- ruäi

The following are the legal effects of divorce or dissolution of marriage:

(1) Relief of the spouses of their mantal relationships.

(2) Freedom of the woman to marry another man.

(3) Recovery of bridewealth cattle or property and offspring and all other rights due to the husband from his wife's Relatives.

(4) Recovery of arueth' and all other rights due to the Relatives of the divorced woman from the husband and his Relatives.

(5) Right of the husband to take the children, provided that he pays aruok'cattle to the Relatives of his divorce wife.

Section 42
Impregnation of a girl "Lienye-Nya"

(a) Whenever a girl is impregnated, the man who has committed the offence is bound to pay a heifer as aruok' to her Relatives or parents, if he refuses to marry her, provided that the heifer shall not be paid by him as aruok, when her relatives refuse to marry her to him, while he is able and ready to satisfy their demand by paying a amount of cattle as bridewealth.

86

(b) Possession of the heifer, which has been obtained as aruok, for the impregnation of the girl is vested in her Relatives, provided that they shall transfer it, together with the girl, to any man who subsequently marries her.

Section 43
Payment of Aruok for a child when a girl is impregnated

When a man impregnates a gin, he shall be given an opportunity to redeem the child, who is the product of such impregnation by paying aruok cattle to the gin's Relatives, otherwise she and her child will be given to any man who will marry her.

Section 44
Elopement with a girl "Jote-nye"

A man who elopes with a girl is bound to pay one heifer to her Relatives as "awac", if the refuses to marry her, provided that he shall not be bound to pay a heifer as "awac" if he is rejected from marrying her by her Relatives on grounds other than failure to pay a sufficient amount of cattle as bridewealth.

Section 45
Penalty where a girl is eloped with for the second time

When a man elopes with a girl for the second tone after he has been rejected from marrying her for failure to pay a sufficient amount of cattle demanded by her Relatives or for some other reasons, he shall only be liable to any penalty provided by the Sudan Penal Code.

Section 46
Transfer of 'awac' heifer to a subsequent husband

The title to any heifer which has been obtained by Relatives as awac' for the elopement with their girl shall be transferred, together with the girl, to any man who will subsequently marry her.

Section 47
Payment of cows for 'tiop' for the death of a married woman

(a) A man whose wife dies naturally shall pay to her relatives or parents two cows and one bull as tiop', when the marriage is deemed to have been dissolved by such death.

(b) The basis for the payment of cattle as tiop is consolation of her parents or relative.

Section 48
Rape "Make - piny"

When a man rapes:

(a) A girl who is

(i) Under age. he is bound to pay to her Relatives five cows as aruok' and he shall also be liable to any penalty which is prescribed by the Sudan Penal Code;

(ii) Mature, he is bound to pay only one heifer to her Relatives as 'aruok' and he shall also be liable to any penalty prescribed by the Sudan Penal Code;

(b) A married woman, he is bound to pay six cows and one bull as aruok' to the husband or his successor and he shall be liable to any penalty prescribed by the Sudan Penal Code;

(c) A free woman, he shall be liable to any penalty prescribed by the Sudan Penal Code.

Section 49
Where a girl or a free woman is impregnated through rape (Lienye-nyan ci makpiny ku ting ci makpiny)

When a girl or a free woman becomes pregnant through rape, the child, born as a result, may belong to the biological father, provided that he redeems him or her by payment of 'aruok' cattle to the gin's or woman's Relatives, otherwise the child may be delivered together with the girl or woman to any man who will formally marry her or marry her with the consent of her parents or Relatives at any time afterwards.

Section 50
Rape cattle transferable to a subsequent husband

The title to the cattle paid by the offender as 'aruok' for raping a girlor free woman, shall be transferred with her to a man who will afterwards formally marry her or marry her with the consent of her parents or Relatives.

Section 51
Succession

Where a person, who owns property, dies intestate the following persons shall be the heirs or successors:

(1) Wife and children;

(2) Parents or brothers, if there are no wife and children.

Section 52

Where the person who dies intestate has no wife, children, parents nor brothers, his paternal uncle, if no maternal uncle, shall hold the possession of the property as a trustee. He shall use this property in rnarrying a woman for the deceased and transfer any balance of the said property to the deceased's newly married woman, who shall also hold it partly as a trustee for her children.

CHAPTER 4
THE LAW OF PROPERTY

Section 53
Tracing of cattle property

When divorce or dissolution of marriage takes place, the husband is entitled to trace his cattle or property into the hands of anyone who has acquired possession or title to them from his in-laws through subsequent marriages, provided that he shall only be entitled to recover damages from his in-laws for any cattle or property delivered by them to the third parties through sale or discharge of certain obligations while the marriage was still valid.

Section 54
Damages for cattle, which naturally died after transfer to third parties

Where a dissolution of a marriage or divorce or other relationship takes place, the husband is entitled to recover damages from his in-laws or transferee for any of the bridewealth or other cattle which naturally died, after the transfer of title or possession to any third party by way of sale of discharge of certain obligations or debts, while the marriage or the relationship was still valid. But he is not entitled to recover any damages for any cattle which naturally died in possession of the in-laws or the transferee before the dissolution of the marriage.

Section 55
Tracing of cattle includes their offspring

Tracing of cattle into the hands of anyone, who has acquired possession or title to them, includes their offspring, but it excludes the offspring, which dies through premature birth (athorbei).

Section 56
Transfer of title to property

The true owner is not deprived of his title when possession of such property has been transferred through:

(1) Theft;

(2) Robbery;

(3) Breach of trust;

(4) Deceit or fraud; and

(5) Any other wrongful means.

Section 57
Tracing of property wrongfully transferred

The true owner is entitled to trace any property which has been transferred to any person through one of the ways mentioned in section 56, sub-sections one to five, above.

Section 58
Recovery of damages where property is wrongfully transferred

If the property which has been transferred in any one of the ways mentioned in section 56 (1-5), above, has been destroyed or has perished or got damaged or injured, the true owner is entitled to recover damages against the person who made the wrongful transfer or acquired possession from him.

Section 59
Tracing of title by way of gift

The title to any property which has been transferred to another by way of gift or donation is not traceable, provided that the giver or the donor had a better title against anyone else at the time of the transfer to the donee.

Section 60
Title to gift property reverts to donor on revocation

The title to any property which has been transferred to another by way of gift or donation reverts to the original owner (donor) when revocation of the gift is effected.

Section 61
No tracing of gift property into the hands of third parties

Trace the property given or donated into the hands of anyone who lawfully or in good faith acquires possession or title to it before the revocation is affected, but he is only entitled to recover damages from the donor or the receiver of the gift.

Section 62
Tracing of property transferred to a third party by a finder

The true owner is entitled to trace his property into the hands of anyone who acquires possession whether in good faith or bad faith through a finder.

Section 63
Tracing of property transferred by non-owner

The owner is entitled to trace his property into the hands of anyone who acquires possession in good faith or bad faith from anyone who has no title to lt.

Section 64
Pledge "Amuk' or "Amec'

(a) Amuk' or Amec' (pledge) is any property delivered by a debtor to a creditor as a form of security or guarantee for the repayment of a debt or discharge of an existing obligation.

(b) If the debtor fails completely to repay the dcbt at the time fixed or at the period which the Court may consider to be reasonably long in the circumstances where no fixed period for the discharge of the debt was agreed upon at the time of the contract, the secured creditor is entitled to own the property he possesses as 'amuk'.

Examples of Amuk

(1) 'A' takes a loan of Ls.30 (or a cow) from 'B'. But 'B' insists that a bull or a cow or some other property should be transferred into his possession temporarily as a guarantee for the repayment of the loan or discharge of the obligation on 'A'. 'A' delivers a cow or any property to 'B' to be held by 'B' till the debt is discharged. This cow or property is called 'Amuk'.

(2) Or, 'A' takes a bull from 'B' and promises to give a heifer to 'B' in the near future. However, in order to assure 'B' that the promise shall ultimately be fulfilled, 'A' may deliver a cow into the possession of 'B' on condition that he will recover it after he has fulfilled his obligation by paying a heifer to "B'.

Section 65
Retention of property for ariop 'Lien"

When a person does some work on another's property on the ground that he shall be paid, he is entitled to retain that property till the owner pays hirn for the work done on lt.

Example: 'A' delivers a hoe to 'B', a blacksmith, to sharpen lt. 'A' and 'B' agree that 'A' shall pay 'B' ten piasters for his work. When 'B' has sharpened the hoe, he is entitled to retain lt till he is paid for his work.

Section 66
Pledge or secured creditor or lienee to exercise reasonable care "Ran-amuk"

Any person who retains possession of a cow or other property as 'amuk' (pledge) or any property for the work done on it (lien) is bound to exercise reasonable care for it. If such a cow or property perishes or disappears through his negligence or the negligence of his successor or agent, he is bound to pay damages to the owner, in case of the property held for work done on it: and in case of amuk', the property or cow which has perished or disappeared in his possession through such negligence shall be deemed as full satisfaction of his claim against the debtor.

Illustration in case of 'amuk': A' takes a bull from 'B' on condition that he will pay a heifer to B' in the near future. A' secures the debt by delivering a cow to SB'. Both 'A' and B' agree that the cow will be taken back to A' when A' delivers a heifer to B' in satisfaction of 'Ws claim.

The cow placed into the possession of 'B' is afterwards killed by a crocodile through 'B's negligence. 'B' is not entitled to claim the heifer for the bull which A' has taken from him because 'A' has been discharged from his obligation by the death of his cow through SB's negligence.

CHAPTER 5
TORTS

Section 67
Damages for personal injuries

The Court or Chiefs' Court shall award damages as follows for the loss of:

One eye -	Seven cows.
Two eyes -	Twenty cows.
One leg -	Ten cows.
Two legs -	Twenty cows.
One arm -	Ten cows.
Two arms -	Twenty cows.
One toe -	One cow.
Grievous hurt -	One cow or more according to the gravity of the injury inflicted.
One tooth -	One bull.
Four front teeth -	One cow.
One molar -	One cow.
Complete loss of hearing -	Ten cows.

Section 68
(i) Damages for personal injury caused by one class of domestic animals

When a cow or bull or goat or ram or sheep causes injury to a person, who is not a trespasser, the cow or bull or goat or ram or sheep, which has caused such injury, shall be awarded to the person as damages.

(ii) Damages for personal injuries caused by another class of domestic animals

When an injury is caused to another person, who is not a trespasser, by a cat or dog or horse or donkey or any domestic animal other than those mentioned in paragraph (i) above, the owner is not bound to pay any damages to the victim, unless he knows that the animal has previously shown a dangerous character.

Section 69
Homicide cases "Nake-raan"

'Apuk' or compensation for killing a person while helping a maternal uncle. Where a person kills another in a fight while helping his maternal uncle or uncles, he and his paternal uncles are bound to pay 'apuk' of thirty (30) head of cattle to the relatives of the deceased. But, if the killer lives as the child of his maternal uncles on the ground that his father did not redeem him by the payment of 'aruok' cattle, where divorce had taken place or where marriage had failed to take place in the case of an impregnated girl or girl eloped with, it is the sole duty of his maternal uncles to pay 'apuk' for him.

Section 70
When apuk is payable by killer's relatives of by the whole tribe

When two tribes or more enter into a fight and some people get killed on either side, the payment of apuk' to the Relatives of the deceased person or persons shall be confined to the killers and their Relatives, but where the killer is unknown, the tribe involved in the fight against the deceased's tribe is bound to pay 'apuk' 'Apuk' or compensation is 30 cows for causing the death of a person.

Section 71
Self- defense is no excuse for avoiding payment of 'apuk'

A person who has caused the death of another is bound with his Relatives on the paternal side to pay 'apuk' of thirty (30) cows to the Relatives of the deceased, although death might have been caused while the killer was exercising the right of self-defense.

Section 72
Apuk and bridewealth properly payable to the husband's Relatives when killed by his wife

If a woman intentionally causes the death of her husband, the marriage is automatically dissolved and the Relatives of the deceased are entitled to obtain 'apuk' cattle together with the cattle they had paid for bridewealth during the marriage from her Relatives, provided that, if there arc children, the deceased Relatives are bound to pay 'aruok' cattle to her Relatives for each child, otherwise her parents or Relatives shall be entitled to take the children.

Section 73
Bridewealth cattle convertible info 'apuk' cattle when husband kills his wife

When a husband intentionally kills his wife, the marriage is dissolved and the cattle which he had paid to her Relatives as bridewealth cattle shall be converted into 'apuk' cattle, but if the amount of the bridewealth cattle he had paid was less than thirty (30) head of

cattle, he and his Relatives arc bound to fill the gap by paying more cattle. However, if the amount of bridewealth cattle was more than thirty (30) head of cattle, he or his suceessor is entitled to red over the surplus from the deceased's Relatives, provided that he or his successor shall pay 'aruok' cattle for each child together with the 'arueth' cattle or any rightful claims to the Relatives of the deceased.

Section 74
Apuk is ten (10) cows when a person is killed through mistake of fact

Where a person kills another through a mistake of fact (rol), he is bound to pay ten (10) cows as 'apuk' to the Relatives of the deceased.

Section 75
Apuk is ten (10) cows where a person is killed by one who lacks capacity or who is insane

Where a person is killed by another who is insane or lunatic, or a child who lacks capacity, the Relatives of the killer arc bound to pay ten (10) cows as 'apuk' to the Relatives of the deceased.

Section 76
Apuk is thirty (30) head of cattle when a relative other than a member of the same family is killed.

Where a person intentionally causes the death of his Kinsman other than a member of his family, he is bound to pay thirty (30) head ofcattle as apuk' to the Relatives of the deceased, unless the members of the deceased's family waive their rights.

Section 77
Apuk is payable by the husband and his Relatives if his wife kills another person

Where a married woman kills another person, who is not her husband's Kinsman, 'apuk' must be paid to the Relatives of the deceased by her husband and his Relatives. But if the marriage between such a woman and her husband is afterwards dissolved, the husband shall be entitled to recover from her Relatives the cattle he had paid as bridewealth together with damages for the thirty (30) head of cattle he had paid for the 'apuk' provided that he shall at the same time be bound to settle all other rights claimed against him by her Relatives.

Section 78
Damages for Defamation (Lete-guop, yor-guop, buol or yuop-buol)

Any person whose reputation is affected or is likely to be affected by the publication of a defamatory statement or injurious falsehood is entitled to recover damages from the wrongdoer as follows:

(i) if the defamatory statement or injurious falsehood is published in an ordinary conversation or talking, he is entitled to obtain one heifer;

(ii) if the falsehood or defamatory statement is published in a song, he is entitled to obtain one pregnant heifer, provided that the Court may pass, in addition, an appropriate sentence of imprisonment or fine or both against him, in accordance with the provisions of the Sudan Penal Code.

Section 79
Damages to properly

When the property of anyone is damaged by (i) a cow or bull, or (ii) a goat or a he-goat, or (iii) a sheep or a ram, which belongs to another person, the owner of the property is entitled to obtain damages from the owner of such animal in the form of money calculated according to the degree of damage done.

Section 80

When a cow or bull or goat or he-goat or sheep or ram dies owing to the injury caused, while it was within the owner's premises, by another trespassing or wandering cow or bull or goat or sheep or ram or he-goat that belongs to another person, the animal that inflicted the injury which caused the death shall be awarded to the owner of the animal which has been killed as damages, but no damages shall be awarded if the injury was caused while both animals were wandering outside the premises of their owners or when trespassing in the premises of a third party.

Section 81
Property destroyed by fire caused by another person

When the property of anyone is destroyed by fire caused by another person, damages shall be awarded to the owner against the tort-feasor in the form of money or a bull or heifer or cow or more, according to the value of the property destroyed or damaged.

PART 3
THE CODE OF LUO CUSTOMARY LAW

Section 82
Title
This Law shall be called the Code of the Luo Customary Law.

Section 83
The provisions of Part 3 shall apply throughout Bahr El-Ghazal Region to:

(1) All Jo-Luo of Bahr El-Ghazal Region.

(2) All persons involved in sexual wrongs with Luo girls, wornen or wives of Bahr El-Gha.zal Region.

(3) Matters connected with marriage, divorce, custody and redemption of children of a Luo woman.

(4) Tortious acts committed within Bahr El-Ghazal Region against a Nga Luo by a non-Luo or by a Nga-Luo outside this Region against a Luo.

CHAPTER 6

Section 84
General explanation and definitions
Sense of expression once explained every expression, which is explained in any part of this Code, is used in every part of this Code in conformity with the explanation, unless the subject or sense of the context otherwise requires.

Section 85
Jogo
'Jogo' or bridewealth is the property payable by the bride-groom and his family to the family of the bride in consideration of her marriage.

Section 86
Reciprocal payment "Arueth"

'Arueth' means the cattle payable by the family of the bride to the bride groom in a certain proportion to the bridewealth.

Section 87
Per or Aruok

'Per' or 'Aruok' is the compensation payable by the male offender in sexual wrongs, namely adultery, fornication, rape and failed elopement.

Section 88
Cimonyo

Cimonyo is the personal token gift made by the bridegroom to the eldest paternal uncle and aunt and eldest sister of the bride, and is currently Ls.20 each. This practice prevails only among the Luo of East Bank of River Jur.

Section 89
Family

Family is what is known in Luo as 'dho uot'.

Section 90
Brothers and Sisters

The terms brothers and sisters include stepbrothers and stepsisters.

Section 91
Girl or woman "Nyakou"

The term nyakou' or girl or woman means an unmarried female of any age.

Section 92
Wife 'Dhango'

Dhango' or wife means a married woman within the provisions of this Code.

Section 93 Husband

Husband means the person married to a woman within the provisions of this Code.

Section 94
Court

Court carries the same meaning as is defined in Part 1 of this Act.

CHAPTER 7
PERSONAL LAW

Section 95
Marriage Definition

(i) Marriage is a union between one man or his successor on his behalf and one or more women for their lives for the purpose of sexual co-habitation, procreation of the young and maintenance of the homestead.

(ii) It shall also be considered marriage, where a parent or a childless woman takes another woman for the purpose of procreation of the young in her name by a consort of her choice.

Section 96
Consent in marriage

The only consent which is material and essential for the conclusion of a valid marriage is that of the families of the spouses. Wherever a man and a woman have taken each other as husband and wife without the prior consent of their families, such a union may be dissolved or confirmed by such families.

Section 97
Consummation of marriage

No marriage shall be consummated between a boy and a girl until both of them have attained maturity.

Section 98
Bridewealth

(1) The families of both parties to a marriage shall be free to fix the amount, amount and kind of bridewealth as well as the manner and time of delivery.

(2) Provided that where the Court marries the parties irrespective of family consent the bridewealth shall be:

(a) Among the Luo of the East Bank of River Jur, 5 cows, 3 bulls, Ls. 600, 15 goats and 12 spears, and 'arueth' is payable;

(b) Among the Luo who have adopted the tradition of marrying in cattle, 30 head of cows and 6 bulls.

Section 99
Contribution to bridewealth

The father, and in his absence, the eldest brother or paternal uncle of the bridegroom is liable to contribute to the payment of bridewealth.

Section 100
Share in bridewealth

(1) The bridewealth goes to the family of the girl to be used as the family thinks fit.

(2) Provided that among the Luo of the East Bank of River Jur. the eldest paternal uncle and aunt and the eldest sister are entitled to 'cimonyo' which is Ls.20.

(3) Provided that among the Luo of the West Bank of River Jur. the eldest maternal uncle is entitled to a cow and the mothers of the parents-in-law are each entitled to one big he-goat.

Section 101
Forms of Marriage

(1) Open courting, engagement to marry, agreement to the marriage and the bride going to live in the house of the bridegroom after the delivery of the bridewealth.

(2) Registration in Court that an agreement has been made to marry the parties and part of the bridewealth has been delivered.

(3) Taking of the woman by the man after an agreement to marry has been made and part of bridewealth delivered.

(4) Elopement which is confirmed.

Section 102
Rights accruing to the man upon marriage

The following nights shall accrue at the outset of the marriage to the husband:

(a) Right to children born during the subsistence of his marriage;

(b) Right to children born out of any wedlock before his marriage;

(c) Right to compensation for fornication by his wife;

(d) Right to compensation for adultery by his wife.

Section 103
Obligations of the husband

The husband is vicariously liable for the torts of his wife and minor children.

Section 104
Sexual wrongs

Adultery: Definition and compensation

(1) Sexual intercourse with a married woman is adultery.

(2) Compensation payable by the adulterer shall be Ls. 100.000 m/ms.

(3) Compensation for adultery shall be payable to the husband, his agent or successor.

Section 105
Fornication: definition and compensation

(1) Sexual intercourse with an unmarried woman is fornication.

(2) Compensation for fornication payable by the fornicator shall be Ls. 50.

(3) Compensation for fornication is payable to the father of the woman in trust for her subsequent husband or her subsequent husband, his agent or successor.

Section 106
Elopement: definition and its results

(1) Elopement is the taking of an unmarried woman with a genuine intention to marry her.

(2) The families of the parties may dissolve or confirm the marnage by elopement.

(3) Where the marriage by elopement is confirmed, the husband shall pay to the family or his wife damages known awaga to be fixed by the family.

(4) Where the marriage by elopement is dissolved the man shall pay compensation as that for adultery.

(5) The Court may confirm the marriage by elopement, irrespective of the opinions of the families of the parties, where it thinks fit and, here, bridewealth is as provided in section 98(2) of the Code.

Section 107
Rape: definition and compensation

(1) Whoever has sexual intercourse with an immature girl or a woman without her consent or against her will is said to have committed rape.

(2) Compensation payable by the rapist shall be:

    (a) In the case of an immature gin, the same as that for an unmarried woman;

    (b) In the case of an unmarried woman, Ls. 150;

    (c) In the case of a married woman, Ls. 200.

(3) Compensation payable for raping an immature girl or unmarried woman shall be recoverable by her father in trust for the subsequent husband of the girl or woman.

(4) Compensation for raping a married woman shall be recoverable by her husband, his agent or successor.

Section 108
Incest: definition and its results

(1) Sexual intercourse with a blood Kinsman is incest.

(2) No compensation is payable for incest, hut the offender shall be liable to punishment.

Section 109
Impregnation of a girl

(1) Compensation for impregnating a girl shall be Ls. 100.

(2) The compensation shall be recoverable by her father or guardian in trust for her subsequent husband.

Section 110
Divorce

When it takes effect

(1) Divorce takes effect upon pronouncement by the Court; or

(2) When the wife leaves her husband and her family returns to the family of the husband the bridewealth, less deductions.

Section 111
Grounds for divorce

The Court may, if it thinks fit, grant divorce on any of the following grounds:

(1) Barrenness of the wife;

(2) Repeated infidelity of the wife;

(3) Neglect of duties by the wife;

(4) Gross misconduct by the wife;

(5) Impotence of the husband;

(6) Gross misconduct by the husband and neglect of his duties.

(7) Total breakdown of the marriage relationship.

Section 112
Parties to divorce suit

The parties to a divorce suit shall be the husband on the one hand, and the wife and her family as co-parties on the other hand.

(1) Upon divorce, the husband shall be entitled to recover the bridewealth paid.

(a) Where there arc no children, all the bridewealth, less an amount equal to compensation for adultery;

(b) Among the Luo of the East Bank of River Jur: where there is only one child, only one (1) cow and cash payment;

(c) Among the Luo of East Bank of River Jur: (i) where there is a girl, four (4) cows and (2) bulls arc deducted; (ii) where there is a boy, three (3) cows and one (1) bull are deducted;

(d) Where the marriage was according to cattle marriage tradition, the Code of the Dinka Customary Law shall apply;

(e) Where there are more than two children, no bridewealth is recoverable.

(2) Upon divorce the family of the woman shall be entitled to:

(a) Recover any compensation received by the husband for rape or fornication or adultery by the wife;

(b) The right to the children until redeemed by the father where the bridewealth paid is not enough to cover the compensation for co-habitation and deductions for the children.

(3) Upon divorce the wife shall have the right to custody of the children until each one attains the age of seven, provided the husband shall be entitled to their custody at an earlier age, if the interest of the children so requires.

Section 114
Liability of husband for children raised by the family of the wife

Where the children arc raised by the family of their mother owing to the neglect of their father to redeem or raise them, the father shall be liable to pay one cow for each child, upon redeeming or collecting them.

Section 115
Effect of death of husband or wife upon marriage

(1) The death of the husband has no effect on the marriage.

(2) The family of the husband may dissolve the marriage upon the death of the wife.

(3) Where the marriage is dissolved due to the death of the wife:

(a) The family of the husband shall be liable to pay to the family of the wife one cow as compensation;

(b) The bridewealth shall be recoverable as upon divorce.

Section 116
Testate succession

A man may, by oral or written will, distribute his property within the family.

Section 117
Intestate succession

(1) The subjects of succession arc:

(a) wife or wives; (b) children; (c) property.

(2) The closest male Relativesinherit the deceased's property generally.

(3) The wives shall be taken over by the male members of the family as they think fit.

(4) Where the deceased left no son or wife his property shall be held in trust

CHAPTER 8
THE LAW OF PROPERTY

Section 118
Interest in land and the right of cultivation

The family has the exclusive right of cultivation on traditional family habitats.

Section 119
Hunting right

The right of the first person to spear an animal:

The first person to spear an animal is the lawful owner of the animal even if killed eventually by another person, provided the person who kills the animal eventually shall be entitled to one of the animal's front legs.

Section 120
Tracing of cattle

Same as in Section 53 of Part 2.

Section 121
Damages for cattle which die naturally after their transfer to a third party

Same as in Section 54 of Part 2.

Section 122
Tracing of off-spring of cattle

Same as in Section 55 of Part 2.

Section 123
Transfer of tide to property

Same as in Section 56 of Part 2.

Section 124
Tracing of property wrongfully transferred
Same as in Section 57 of Part 2.

Section 125
Recovery of damages where property is wrongfully transferred
Same as in Section 58 of Part 2.

Section 126
Transfer of property by way of gift
Same as in Section 59 of Part 2.

Section 127
Tide to gift property reverts to donor on revocation
Same as in Section 60 of Part 2.

Section 128
No tracing of gift property into die hands of third parties
Same as in Section 61 of Part 2.

Section 129
Tracing of property transferred to a third party by finder
Same as in Section 62 of Part 2.

Section 130
Tracing of property transferred by non-owner
Same as in Section 63 of Part 2.

Section 131
Pledge
Same as in Section 64 of Part 2.

Section 132
Lien

Same as in Section 65 of Part 2.

Section 133
Pledge and lienee to exercise care

Same as in Section 66 of Part 2.

CHAPTER 10
TORTS

Section 134
Damages for personal injuries

(1) Damages recoverable for the loss of:

    (a) One eye -   two cows and one bull.

    (b) Both eyes -   three cows, two bulls and Ls. 300.

    (c) One leg -   two cows and one bull.

    (d) Both legs -   three cows and one bull.

    (e) One arm -   two cows and one bull.

    (f) Both arms - three cows and one bull.

    (g) Hearing -   two cows and one bull.

(2) Damages recoverable for other personal injuries shall be in accordance with the gravity of the injury inflicted.

Section 135
Damages for personal injury caused by domestic animals

Same as in Section 68 of Part 2.

Section 136
Compensation for causing death

Compensation shall be payable in all cases of causing the death of any person.

Section 137
To whom compensation for causing death shall be payable

(a) The family of the deceased.

(b) The family of his mother, where:

    (i) His mother is not married;

    (ii) He has not been redeemed by his father.

Section 138
Persons liable to pay compensation for causing death

Compensation for causing death shall be payable by

(1) The family of the killer;

(2) The family or clan of the family that was fighting the family or clan of the deceased where the killer is unknown;

(3) The family of the mother of the killer, where:

    (a) His mother is not married;

    (b) He has not been redeemed by his father;

(4) The family of a married woman who has killed and the family of her husband.

Section 139
Compensation payable for causing death by accident or negligence, causing death by a minor or person of unsound mind

(1) Compensation for causing death, unless otherwise provided for herein after, shall be:

    (a) for a childless person, live (5) cows, four (4) bulls and Ls. 500;

    (b) for a person who has a son, three (3) cows, two (2) bulls and Ls. 300.

(2) Compensation for causing death by accident or negligence or by a minor or person of unsound mind shall be two (2) cows and one (1) bull and Ls. 250.

Section 140
Effects of wife killing

Where the husband intentionally kills his wife, he shall be liable:

(a) to complete payment of bridewealth, if not paid in full;

(b) to pay compensation for the death.

Section 141
Where the wife kills the husband intentionally

Where the wife kills the husband intentionally:

(a) the marriage is dissolved;

(b) the family of the wife pays the family of the husband the compensation for causing death.

Section 142
Damages for defamation

Damages are recoverable for defamation published other than in the form of a song.

Section 143
Damage to property by domestic animals

Same as in Section 79 and 80 of Part 2.

Section 144
Damage to property by fire

Where property is destroyed or damaged by fire caused by another, the owner shall be entitled to damages payable by the person who caused the fire.

PART 4
THE CODE OF FERTIT CUSTOMARY LAW

Section 145
Title

This Law shall be called the Code of Fertit Customary Law.

Section 146
Application

The provisions of Part 4 shall apply throughout Bahr El-Ghazal Region to:

(a) All Fertjt of Bahr El-Ghazal Region.

(b) All persons involved in sexual wrongs with Fertit giris, women or wives in Bahr El-Ghazal Region.

(c) Matters connected with marriage, divorce, custody and redemption of children of a Fertit woman.

CHAPTER 10
GENERAL EXPLANATIONS AND DEFINITIONS

Section 147
Sense of expression once explained

Every expression, which is explained in this Code is used in every part of this Code in conformity with the explanation, unless the subject or sense of the content otherwise requires.

Section 148
Mbo ni or Mali ni (Ndogo) vili ni (Balanda)

Mbo ni' or bridewealth is the property payable by the bride-groom and his family to the family of the bride in consideration of her marriage.

Section 149
Ba si co

'Ba si co' is the compensation payable by the male offender in sexual wrong, namely adultery, fornication and rape.

Section 150
Family

'Brother' and 'sister'

(i) The terms 'brother and sister include stepbrother and stepsister.

(ii) 'Vi ni' means unmarried female up to the age of 18 years.

(iii) 'Ni' includes married or unmarried woman.

(iv) 'Ni dako' means a married woman within the provisions of this Code.

(v) 'Mgbanga' Court carries the same meaning as is defined in Part 1 of this amended Act.

CHAPTER
PERSONAL LAW

Section 151
Marriage

Definition of marriage

Marriage is a Union between the families of the spouses for the life of each spouse for the purpose of sexual co-habitation, procreation of the young and maintenance of the homestead.

Section 152
Consent in Marriage

The only consent which is material and essential for the conclusions of a valid marriage is that of the families of the spouses, as well as that of the spouses themselves.

Explanation:

It must be noted that if the girl does not consent to the marriage or is forced to marry the man she does not want, the marriage is very likely to break down, that is why kaaʻ is always put before the elders and the spouse is asked to take it; if she takes it, this symbolizes that she accepts to marry the bride-groom; if she refuses to take it, it means that she does not want him.

Section 153
Consummation of marriage

No marriage shall be consummated between a boy and a girl until both of them have attained maturity.

Section 154
Bridewealth

(a) The Relatives of the two parties shall be free to fix the bridewealth to be paid by the Relatives of the bridegroom to the Relatives of the bride.

Explanation:

(i) The bridewealth is always difficult to fix. It is always the family of the bride who say they want such and such amount to be paid for their gin, and the family of the bridegroom will try to persuade them to reduce it until they eventually agree on what the family of the bridegroom have to pay.

(ii) The current tendency has been that parents of the girls demand high bridewealth, It has been noticed with alarm that this discourages marriages, thus leaving a large amount of unmarried men and women in the community. Therefore, the parents should revert to the age-old practice of demanding low bridewealth.

(b) Bridewealth or ʻmaliniʻ shall be paid by the bridegroom or his father or brother or by the maternal uncle, if he is not a redeemed child, to the bride.

(c) Where a man and a woman agree to cohabit as husband and wife, regardless of the consent of their parents, the father of the girl shall be entitled to sue the man for the bridewealth.

Section 155
Forms of marriage

(1) Open courting.

(2) Sending of 'kaa' by the bride-groom to the family of the spouse to see if the spouse accepts to be married to him or not.

(3) Bride-groom goes openly to his in-law's house and performs any work he may be required to do.

(4) The bride is taken to the house of the bridegroom where a feast for the marriage takes place.

Section 156
Rights accruing to the husband upon marriage

The following rights shall accrue at the outset of the marriage to the husband:

(a) right to children born during the subsistence of the marriage;

(b) right to compensation for the adultery of his wife.

Section 157
Sexual wrongs

Adultery: definition

(a) Sexual intercourse with a married woman is adultery.

(b) Compensation payable by the adulterer shall be Ls. 150 payable to the husband.

Section 158
Rape

Definition and compensation

Whoever has sexual intercourse with an immatured girl or a matured girl or woman without her consent is said to have committed rape.

Compensation payable by the rapist shall be as follows:

(i) For a married woman, Ls.200 payable to her husband.

(ii) For an unmarried wornan, Ls.150 payable to her family.

(iii) For an immatured gin, Ls.300 payable to her parents.

(iv) For a wife of a blood friend Muka or Bakure', one head of tobacco, one white cock and one bow and arrows.

Explanation: lt is the custom of the Fertit that money, molodo', 'kaa', etc., should never be paid between blood friends, because this has been cursed at the time of drinking of blood between the two parties concerned.

Note. The use of tobacco, arrows, bow and white cock is for swearing the two parties, man and woman, not to repeat this again.

Section 159
Divorce
When divorce takes effect

(a) Divorce takes effect upon pronouncement by the Court.

(b) The parties to the divorce suit arc the husband and his wife.

Section 160
Ground for divorce
The Court, if it thinks fit, grants divorce on any of the following grounds:

(1) Repeated infedility of the wife.

(2) Neglect of duties by the wife.

(3) Gross misconduct by the wife.

(4) Gross misconduct by the husband and neglect of his duties to the family.

(5) Impotence of the husband.

(6) Total breakdown of the marriage relationship.

Section 161
Effect of divorce

(1) Where there arc no children, and if the husband is the cause of the divorce, he is returned only his 'kaa' and the bridewealth is retained by the family of the woman.

(2) Where the cause of the divorce is from the wife, and if they have children, the husband is returned half of the bridewealth, all his children plus his 'kaa'.

(3) The woman is returned to her relatives.

(4) Upon divorce the wife shall have the right of custody of the children until they attain the age of seven, provided that the husband shall be entitled to their custody at an earlier age, if the interest of the children so require.

Section 162
Effect of death of husband or wife upon marriage

(1) When the husband dies his wife may remain within the family, provided that she is married by one of his Relatives.

(2) When the wife dies, the husband is still bound to contribute to the unpaid part or balance of the bridewealth to her family.

Section 163
Testate and intestate succession

(1) A man may, by oral or written will, distribute his properties within the family.

(2) Where a man dies without making a will, his estate passes to his children or his brothers or dose Relativesin that order.

CHAPTER 12
THE LAW OF PROPERTY INTEREST IN LAND

Section 164
Right of cultivation

The family has the exclusive right of cultivation and dwelling on traditional family habitats.

Section 165
Hunting right

The person who spears an animal first is the lawful owner of that animal, even if it is eventually killed by another person, provided that the person who eventually kills it is entitled to one front leg of that animal.

Section 166
Transfer of title to property

Same as in Section 56 of Part 2.

Section 167
Tracing of property wrongfully transferred

Same as in Section 57 of Part 2.

Section 168
Recovery of damages where properly is wrongfully transferred

Same as in Section 58 of Part 2.

Section 169
Transfer of title by way of gift

Same as in Section 59 of Part 2.

Section 170
Transfer of property to a third party by finder

Same as in Section 62 of Part 2.

Section 171
Tracing of property that transferred by non-owner
Same as in Section 63 of Part 2.

Section 172
Lien or retention of property for work done on it
Same as in Section 65 of Part 2.

CHIEFS' COURTS ORDINANCE 1931

Nuer courts arc established under the Chiefs' Courts Ordinance 1931, which applies to the three southern Provinces of the Sudan: the Bahr el Ghazal, Equatorial, and the Upper Nile. The Ordinance has been reprinted in The Laws of the Sudan, Supplement to Volume ' pp. 76-81. lt should be noted that this Ordinance has been altered by the terms of the Self Government Statute (1953), section 76, i.e.:

(5) There shall be vested in the Chief Justice all the powers conferred upon the Governor-General . . . by . . . the Chiefs' Courts Ordinance '93'.

(6) There shall further be vested in the Chief Justice all the powers conferred upon Governors by the Chiefs' Courts Ordinance 1931.

Provided that:

(a) The Chief Justice may delegate all or any of the said powers to the Governor concerned;

(b) the Chief Justice may delegate any power, other than the powers of establishing and convening Courts and of appointing Presidents and members of Courts, to the Judge of the Civil High Court of a Province;

(c) Neither the Chief Justice nor a Judge of the Civil High Court shall exercise any of the said powers except after consultation with the Governor concerned.'

As a result of the various constitutional changes which will take place during the next few years, further modifications of the Ordinance may be expected.

Each court is established by warrant under the hand of the Chief Justice which lays down the jurisdiction, constitution, powers, etc., in accordance with the provisions of the Ordinance, but subject to the Regulations which accompany the warrant. A 'Main Court' has jurisdiction over a District or part of a District. For example, the Central Nuer Court has jurisdiction over all tribes in that district including a few small Dinka tribes. In Western Nuer District there arc two Main Courts. A Main Court sits only occasionally, five members in addition to the president forming a quorum, of whom at least two must be presidents of Regional Courts or Magistrates under the Criminal Code of Procedure. There are then a series of 'Regional Courts' within each District. The area over which each Regional Court has jurisdiction corresponds to the territory of a tribe, an amalgamation of tribes, or in some cases, the primary segments of a tribe, although the name of the Regional Court often derives from that of the place at which the court centre is situated. In some districts, there arc also 'Branch Courts' of more limited jurisdiction and powers.

Under section 7 (i) of the Chiefs'Courts Ordinance 1931: A Chief's Court shall administer:

(a) the native law and custom prevailing in the area over which the Court exercises its jurisdiction provided that such native law and custom is not contrary to justice, morality or order;

(b) the provisions of any ordinance which the Court may be authorised to administer in its warrant or regulations.'

Right of appeal is from the court to the District Commissioner or 'to such Chiefs'Courts as the Governor, with the consent of the Governor General (now of the Chief Justice) may authorize to hear appeals'. In most cases appeals from Regional Courts go to a Main Court and only in very exceptional cases to the District Commissioner or higher authority.

Apart from the technicalities of the legal procedure, which the Nuer litigant so often ignores, a civil dispute of the kind already described usually follows a standard course. The dispute is first discussed within the local group or kinship circle and some attempt is made by the elders and headmen to settle it. Up to this point the dispute is ruac cieng, 'home taik'. Failing a settlement the plaintiff refers the case to a Branch or Regional Court and, if dissatisfied with the judgment, then appeals to the Main Court of the District.

THE CONSTITUTION OF CHIEFS' COURTS

The constitution of the Chiefs' Courts, which governs the traditional or customary laws of the people of the Southern Sudan, was established by means of a statutory instrument called the Chiefs' Courts Ordinance, 1931. this was the first time the State machinery got involved in the constitutional organization of the traditional judicial system in the Southern Sudan. S. 4(1) established the Constitution of the Chiefs' Courts as follows:

There shall be the following classes of Chiefs' Courts:

(a) a Chief sitting alone

(b) a Chief as President sitting with members;

(c) s Special Court as provided in S. 8 of the Ordinance.

Chiefs' Courts under (a) and (b) above, are permanently established by means of warrants called the Warrants of Establishments of Courts under the hand of the Chief Justice.

The class of courts under (b) above, has been implemented in the following hierarchy:

(i) a Chiefs' Court called Branch Court (A- Court) with a chief sitting as President with members;

(ii) a Chiefs' Court called Regional Court (B- Court) with a chief sitting as President with members;

(iii) a Chiefs' Court called Main Court, sometimes called Court of Appeal (C –Court); it was later abolished, however.

In the order of seniority, which their powers indicate, the Branch Court is the lowest court, while the Main Court was the highest.

Both the Branch and Regional Courts are only courts of first instance, while the Main Court had the appellate authority.

It was also a court of first instance in major cases in which the other two courts were incompetent in terms of powers to adjudicate.

The jurisdiction of the chiefs' courts is one of the most important subjects of the ordinance. It has been defined as:

- the power of a court or a judge to entertain an action, petition or other proceeding

- the district or limits within which the judgments or orders of a court can be enforced or executed.

REFERENCES

A. A. Kolajo, Customary law in Nigeria through the cases, Ibadan [u.a.], Spectrum Books, 2000.

Aleu Akechak Jok, Robert A. Leitch and Carrie Vandewint, A Study of Customary Law in Contemporary Southern Sudan, Justice, March, 2004.

Arnold-Baker, Charles, Local Council Administration 4th ed., Butterworth, London, 1994.

Allen, Timothy F. H. and Thomas W. Hoekstra, Toward a Unified Ecology, Columbia University Press, New York, 1992.

Anderson, E. N., Ecologies of the Heart: Emotion, Belief and the Environment, Oxford University Press, Oxford, 1996.

Arnold, J. E. M., Management of Forest Resources as Common Property, Commonwealth Forestry Review, vol. 72, p. 157, 1993.

Arrow, Kenneth et al., Economic Growth, Carrying Capacity, and the Environment Science, vol. 268, p. 520, April 28, 1995.

Arthur Phillips, Survey of African Marriage and Family Life, AMS Press. Inc, June 1974.

Austin, J. L., How to do Things with Words (edited by J. 0. Urmson, Oxford University Press, Oxford, 1962.

Ancient laws of Ireland, Ancient Laws of Ireland, 6 Vols. Reprint of the 1865-1901 edition, William S Hein & Co, February 2000.

Arun Agrawal, Dismantling the Divide Between Indigenous and Scientific Knowledge Development and Change, vol. 26, p. 413, University of Florida, 1995.

Bert Carnpbell, Lectures on Jurisprudence or the Philosophy of Positive Law, 4th ed, Thoemmes Press, Reprint Bristol, 1978.

Charles D' Olivier, Matrimonial Laws of the Sudan, 1963.

Charles Lewis Tupper, Punjab Customary law, Office of the Superintendent of Government Print., Calcutta, 1881.

Dias, Jurisprudence, 2nd edition, Butterworths, London, 1964.

D. Greenberg and S. Katz (eds.), Constitutionalism und Democracy, Oxford University Press, Oxford, 1993.

Fergusson, V. H., The Nuong Nuer, S.N.R., Nuer Beast Tales, S.N.R., 1924.

Finnis, John, Natural Law and Natural Rights. Oxford, Clarendon Press., 1980.

Frank Cass, Readings in African Law, Vol. II, London, 1970.

Valentin Aleksandrovic Rjazanovskij, Customary Law of the Mongol tribes, Artistic Printing house, 1929.

H. A. Rose, A Compendium of the Punjab customary law, 2.ed., Lahore, Civil and Military Gazette, 1910-11.

John Scriven, Treatise on the law of copyholds and of the other tenures of lands within manors, Butterworths, London, 1882.

Minh Day, Alternative Dispute Resolution and Customary Law; Resolving Property Disputes in Post Conflict Nations, A Case Study of Rwanda. Georgetown Immigration Law Journal. Fall 2001.

Sir Henry Sumner Maine, Dissertations on Early Law and Custom, John Murray, London, 1883.

E.E. Evans-Pritchard, The Nuer: A Description of the Modes of Livelihood and Political Institutions of a Nilotic People, Oxford University Press, 1940.

Mahmoud A. El-Gamal, Islamic Finance: Law, Economics, and Practice, Cambridge University Press, 2006.

Van Caenegem , English law suits from William I to Richard I, R.C., 2 vol., London, 1990-1991.

Gillette, Clayton P., Rules and Reversibility, Notre Dame Law, 1997.

Gleick, James, Faster, The Acceleration of Just About Everything, Pan New York, 1999.

Gough, J. W., Fundamental Law in English Constitutional History, Oxford Press, Oxford, 1955.

Grafton, R. Quentin, Dale Squires and Kevin J. Fox, Private Property and Efficiency: A Study of a Common-Pool Resource, Journal Economics, vol. 43, p. 679., 2000.

Green, Thomas Hill, Lectures on the Principles of Political Obligation London, 1895.

Grossi, Paolo, An Alternative to Private Property, University of Chic Chicago, 1981.

Grotius, Hugo, The Freedom of the Seas (translated by Magoffin), Oxford Press, Oxford, 1916.

Guy, Richard K., "The Strong Law of Small Amount American M. Monthly, vol. 95, p. 697.

Marion R. Chertow and Daniel C. Esty (eds.), Thinking, The Next Generation of Environmental Policy, Yale University Press, 1997.

Haavelmo, Trygve, A Study in the Theory of Economic Evolution. Section I of Grabbing, Protection and Cooperation (North Holland Publishing Amsterdam, 1954.

Henry Sumner Maine, Village Communities in the East and West. London, John Murray, pp. 64-128. 1881.

Howell, P. P 'A Note on Elephants and Elephant Hunting among the Nuer, S.N.R., '945.

Hudson, A., Equity and Trusts (3rd ed.), Cavendish Publishing, 2003.

Effa Okupa, International bibliography of African customary law: ius non-scriptum, Hamburg: Lit, 1998.

Mark E. Villiger, Customary international law and treaties: a manual on the theory and practice of the interrelation of sources (Fully rev. 2. ed), The Hague, Kluwer Law Internat., 1997.

Richard B. Lillich , Customary international human rights law : evolution, status and future ; papers from the 1994 colloquium, The University of Georgia School of Law, Athens, Ga., 1996.

Nancy Kontou, The termination and revision of treaties in the light of new customary international law, Clarendon Press, Oxford, 1994.

Marjorie Mandelstam Balzer, Russian traditional culture: religion, gender, and customary law, NY Sharpe, 1992.

Jan C. Bekker, Seymour's customary law in southern Africa, 5. ed., 2. impr., Cape Town, Juta, 1991

Robert B. Serjeant, Customary and Shari'ah law in Arabian society, London: Variorum, 1991.

Hungdah Chiu, The status of customary international law, treaties, agreements and semi-official or unofficial agreements in Chinese law, Baltimore, Md. : School of Law, Univ. of Maryland, 1989.

John W. Makec, The customary law of the Dinka people of Sudan: in comparison with aspects of western and Islamic laws, London: Afro-world Publ, 1988.

Eugene Cotran, Casebook on Kenya customary law, Abingdon : Professional Books [u.a.], 1987.

Barthazar Aloys Rwezaura, State law and customary law : reflections on their relationship in contemporary Tanzania; Vortrag vor d. Europa-Inst. d. Univ. d. Saarlandes, Saarbruecken, 3. Juni 1987.

Mark E. Villiger, Customary international law and treaties: a study of their interactions and interrelations with special consideration of the 1969 Vienna Convention of the Law of Treaties, Dordrecht [u.a.] : Nijhoff, 1985.

The construction and transformation of African customary law London: School of Oriental and African Studies, Univ., 1984.

Paul Heinrich Neuhaus, International encyclopedia/ Vol. 4, Chapter 11, The family in religious and customary law, 1983.

Gewohnheitsrecht und ländliche Entwicklung in Afrika : d. Einfluß d. Customary Land Tenure Law auf d. Entwicklungsprozeß u.d. Bodenrechtsreform am Beisp. Sierra Leones / Kurt H. Ebert. - München [u.a.] : Weltforum Verl., 1982.

Ibrahim M. Atai, A dictionary of the terminology of Pashtun's tribal customary law and usages, Kabul: Internat, Centre for Pashto Studies, Acad. of Sciences of Afghanistan, 1979.

James P. MacGough, Marriage and adoption in Chinese society with special reference to customary law, 1976.

H. W. A. Thirlway, International customary law and codification, Leiden, 1972.

Richard J. Erickson, International law and the revolutionary state, Dobbs Ferry, N.Y., Oceana Publ., 1972.

John Henry Wigmore, Law and justice in Tokugawa. / Pt. 7 / Persons : civil customary law, 1972.

Hans Cory, Customary law of the Haya tribe, Tanganyika Territory, London, 1971.

John Henry Wigmore, Law and justice in Tokugawa, civil customary law, 1971.

Abdulla M. A. Maktari, Water rights and irrigation practices in Lah☒j, a study of the application of customary and Shariah law in south-west Arabia, Cambridge University Press, 1971.

Paul Philip Howell, A manual of Nuer law, (Reprint) Publ. for the International African Institute, Oxford Univ. Pr., London 1970.

Richard Olufemi Ekundare, Marriage and divorce under Yoruba customary law, Ibadan, Univ. of IFE Pr., 1969.

Max Gluckman, Ideas and procedures in African customary law, studies presented and discussed at the Eighth International African Seminar at the Haile Sellassie I. University, Addis Ababa, London, Oxford Univ. Press, 1969.

Johan Frederik Holleman, Shona customary law: with reference to kinship, marriage, the family and the estate, Manchester Univ. Press, 1969.

Zdenek J. Slouka, International custom and continental shelf, The Hague: Nijhoff, 1968.

David C. Buxbaum, Family law and customary law in Asia: a contemporary legal perspective, The Hague, Nijhoff, 1968.

Frank M. Mifsud, Customary land law in Africa : With reference to legislation aimed at adjusting customary tenures to the needs of development /. - Rome : Food and Agriculture Organization of the United Nations, 1967.

William Henry, Sir Rattigan, A digest of civil law for the Punjab,14. ed., rev. by Harbans Lal Sarin and Kundan Lal Pandit, Allahabad: Univ. Book Agency, 1966.

Valentin A. Riasanovsky, Customary law of the nomadic tribes of Siberia /. - Bloomington, Ind. : Indiana Univ. [u.a.], 1965.

Jacob Cornelis Vergouwen, The social organisation and customary law of the Toba-Batak of Northern Sumatra, The Hague : Nijhoff, 1964.

Nil Amaa Ollennu, Principles of customary land law in Ghana, Londo, Sweet & Maxwell, 1962.

 The future of customary law in Africa Leiden, Univ. Pers, Leiden, 1956

Taslim Olawale Elias, The Nature of African customary law, Manchester, Manchester Univ. Pr., 1956.

Louis J. Luzbetak And Vienna-Modling, Marriage and the family in Caucasia, a contribution to the study of North Caucasian ethnology and customary law, St. Gabriel's Mission Press, 1951.

Ways and means of making the evidence of customary international law more readily available Lake Success, N.Y.: (United Nations), 1949

Valentin Aleksandrovic Rjazanovskij, Customary Law of the nomadic tribes of Siberia, Tientsin, [London: K. Paul, 1938.

Kaikhusrau Jahangir Rustamji, A Treatise on customary law in the Punjab, 3. rev. ed., Lahore: Univ. Book Agency, 1936.

Leonhard Adam, The social Organization and customary law of the Nepalese tribes, Washington, 1936.

Robert D. Cooter, Issues in Customary Land Law, University of California at Berkeley, 1989.

Jackson, H. C., The Nuer of the Upper Nile Province, S.N.R., 1923.

Jeffery, Clarence Ray, The Development of Crime in Early English Society, Journal of Criminal Law, Criminology, and Police Science, 1957.

John Austin, Wilfrid E. Rumble, The Province of Jurisprudence Determined (Weidenfeld & Nicc, London, 1954.

John Henry Merryman, Civil Law Tradition: Introduction to the Legal Systems of Western Europe and Latin America, Stanford U.P. February 1970.

Karsten, Peter, Between Law and Custom, Cambridge University Press, Cambridge, 2002.

Jochen Hippler, The Democratisation of Disempowerment in Africa, The Democratisation of Disempowerment, Pluto Press, London, 1995.

Keiter, Robert B., Beyond the Boundary Line: Constructing a Law of Ecosystem Management University of Colorado Law Review, vol. 65, p. 293, 1994.

ken, Paul, The Ecology of Commerce: A Declaration of Sustainability, Harper Collins Business, New York, 1994.

Kiggen, Fr. J., Nuer-English Dictionary, 1948.

Tomoya Kimichi, "Indigenous Resource Management and Sustainable Development: Case Studies from Papua New Guinea and Indonesia, Anthropological Science, vol. 103, p. 321, Anthropological Society of Nippon, 1995.

Kingdon, F. D., 'The Western Nuer Patrol, 1927-28', S.N.R., 1945.

Kinship and Local Community among the Nuer, in African Systems of Kinship and Marriage (cd. Forde and Radcliffe-Brown),1950.

Kur, Dengtiel. A., Access to Traditional Justice Systems & the Rights of Women and Children in South Sudan. Workshop on the Legal Protection of Children Organized by the South Sudan Law Society, Rumbek, New Sudan. At 2., 2000.

Kur, Dengtiel. A., Customary Law and Access to Justice in South Sudan.

Abdel Salem, A. H., Phoenix State: Civil Society and the Future of Sudan, Red Sea Press, 2001.

Peter Ørebech, Fred Bosselman, Jes Bjarup, David Callies, Martin Chanock, Hanne Petersen, The Role of Customary Law in Sustainable Development, Cambridge University Press, 2005

Petherick, Mr. and Mrs. J., Travels in Central Africa, 1869.

Poncet, Jules, 'Le Fleuve Blanc', extrait des Nouvelles Annales des Voyages, Paris, 1863.

Prina, M., '11 Segno distintive nazionale dei Nuer', La Nigrizia, 1935.

Redaelli, E., 'Fra i Nuer', La Nigrizia, 1926.

Reports of the Jonglei Investigation Team, 1946 to 1953 (Sudan Govern ment).

Richard, "Traditional Aboriginal Land Use: Wisdom for Sustainable Development (Australian National University Centre for Resource and Environmental Studies, Canberra, 19 - Edward B., et al., Paradise Lost: The Ecological Economics Publications, London, 1994.

Robert Axelrod, The Evolution of Cooperation (Basic Books, New York, 1 Edward et al., "International Ecosystem Assessment (October 22, ience, vol. 286, p. 685.

Robert Carson Allen, "The Efficiency and Distributional Consequences of Eighteenth Century Enclosures The Economics Journal vol 92 p 937., 1982.

Sir Henry Sumner Maine Ancient Law: Its Connection with the Early History of Society and its Relation to Modern Ideas, Theommes Press, reprint Bristol, London 1861.

Sripati Charan Roy, Customs and customary law in British India, Hare press, 1911.

Seligman, C. G. and B. Z., Pagan Tribes of the Nilotic Sudan, 1932.

Short History of Sudan by Mohamed H., Dr. Fadlalla, iUniverse, NY, USA, 2004.

Sir Edward Coke and the Elizabethan Age: Savagery and Civilization in Paris and the South Pacific, 1790-1900 (Jurists--Profiles in Legal Theory), Alice Bullard , Allen D. Boyer, Stanford Uni. Press, December 2000.

Sir Henry Maine: A Study in Victorian Jurisprudence (Cambridge Studies in English Legal History) von Raymond Cocks, R. C. J. Cocks, und John H. Baker von Cambridge University Pr - 30. September 2004.

Stigand, C. H., 'Warrior Ciasses of the Nuers', S.N.R., 1918.

The Anthropology of Law and Issues of Justice in the Southern Sudan Today, A Thesis submitted to University of Oxford in partial fulfillment of the requirements of Master of Philosophy in Social Anthropology (2000), Administration of Justice in the SPLM Liberated Areas: Court Cases in War-Torn Southern Sudan, Refugee Studies Programme, University of Oxford, (1997), and Save Our Customary Laws Now, 1997.

The Casus Placitorum and reports of cases in the King's Court, 1271-1278, W.H. Dunham, London 1950.

The Concept of Law, Studies in Jurisprudence and Political Theory, 2nd ed., Oxford University Press, Oxford.

Howard M. Hensel, The legitimate use of military force, The just war tradition and the customary law of armed conflict, Aldershot, Ashgate, 2008.

Elizabeth Wilmshurst, Perspectives on the ICRC study on customary international humanitarian law, Cambridge, Cambridge University Press 2007.

Mohsen Aghahosseini, Claims of dual nationals and the development of customary international law, issues before the Iran-United States Claims Tribunal, Leiden, 2007.

Przemysław Paul Polański, Customary law of the internet: in the search for a supranational cyberspace law, The Hague : T. M. C. Asser Press, c 2007.

Amanda Perreau-Saussine, The nature of customary law, Cambridge [u.a.]: Cambridge Univ. Press, 2007.

Jo-Anne Fiske, Seeking alternatives to Bill C-31 : from cultural trauma to cultural revitalization through customary law, Ottawa : Status of Women Canada, 2006.

Jo-Anne Fiske, The Nature of Democracy in Popular Government Jo-Anne Fiske, London, 1886.

Sayyid Muhammad Abu Rannat, The Relationship between Islamic and Customary Law in the Sudan",. Journal of African Law, Vol. 4, No. 1 1960.

Manfred Otto Hinz, The shade of new leaves : governance in traditional authority ; a southern african perspective ; [International Conference on the Living Reality of Customary Law and Traditional Governance held in Windhoek in 2004 ... organised by the Centre for Applied Social Sciences ...]/. - Muenster [u.a.] : LIT, 2006.

Peter Ørebech, The right and duty of states to prosecute torture committed abroad amongst foreigners : universal jurisdiction over torture under customary international law and the UN Convention against Torture / Claire Annette Hubert, Oslo, Institutt for Offentlig Rett, Univ. i Oslo, 2005

The role of customary law in sustainable development, Cambridge [u.a.]: Cambridge Univ. Press, 2005.

Todd Weiler, International investment law and arbitration: leading cases from the ICSID, NAFTA, bilateral treaties and customary international law, London, 2005.

Jean-Marie Henckaerts, Customary international humanitarian law, Cambridge [u.a.] : Cambridge Univ. Press, 2005.

Uwe Mehlitz, Die Stellung des Customary law im Zivilrechtspluralismus Namibias, Baden-Baden, Nomos Verl.-Ges., 2004.

Adino Vitso, Customary law and women: the Chakhesang Nagas, New Delhi: Regency Publications, 2003.

Thomas V. McClendon, Genders and generations apart: labor tenants and customary law in segregation-era South Africa, 1920s to 1940s, Portsmouth, NH, Heinemann, 2002.

Mariano Garcia-Rubio, On the application of customary rules of state responsibility by the WTO dispute settlement organs: a general international law perspective, Genève : IUHEI, 2001.

Leon Shaskolsky Sheleff, The future of tradition: customary law, common law, and legal pluralism, London, Cass, 2000.

Tom G, On customary law and the Saami rights process in Norway: proceedings from a conference at the University of Tromsø, Feb. 1999.

Endnotes

1   Tribal Chief by Nuer is the Leopard- skin Chief, it supposed that he acts as political agent rather than an agent with a judicial authority, although in Zeraf tribes, the Leopard- Skin Chief usually had powerful kinsmen, and the majority of tribal segments Leopard -Skin families were represented in the dominant lineage. see: a Manual of Nuer Law, p 29.

2   Further efforts followed after independence regarding Dinka customary law in 1970th, which resulted in what came to be known as Wanh-Alel Code. The efforts to improve application of customary laws intensified after the signing of the Peace Agreement. A Customary Law Steering Committee (CLSC) was established.

A recommendation to establish a centre on Customary Law issues were made during the Legal Institutions and Law Enforcement Agencies Conference held at Himan New Kush in April 1999. The issue arose again in late 2003 during the Justice and Security Sector workshop held at Rumbek. More recently, during the Joint Assessment Mission (JAM) it was agreed under Cluster II workshop held at Rumbek in October 2004, that Customary Law was a crosscutting issue affecting various departments of the New Sudan.

Once established, the Customary Law Steering Committee (CLSC) organized a consultative workshop with the following objectives:

1. Bringing together key stakeholders involved in the research and documentation of Customary Law in the South Sudan to share information and experiences.

2. Identifying and prioritizing the planning phases for the ascertainment of Customary Law regimes in South Sudan.

3. Developing strategies for the collection, storage and use of existing research materials on Customary Law

4. Identifying and agreeing upon the resources that are required to implement the outcomes of the workshop

The workshop was organized around the following themes:

1. Historical development of Customary Law

2. Information and experience sharing

3. Ascertainment and Documentation of Customary Law

4. Institutional support and development for the CLSC

See: Workshop Report of the First Customary Law Work Plan Workshop, SPLM Secretariat for Legal affairs and Constitutional Development (SOLA), Customary Law Steering Committee (CLSC) Held at Nairobi (14th- 16th December 2004.). The participants were many, some with interest on customary law and similar running project like Norwegian Peoples Aid, which has project on Customary Law on land tenure systems. Others like Max Planck Institute for International Law, the World Vision International, Sudanese Women Association in Nairobi (SWAN), South Sudan Law Society, FAO and the Christian Aid participants pronounced interest and also their believe that Customary Law has huge potential for conflict resolution. The workshop recognized the importance of ascertainment of Customary Law and acknowledged that Customary Law has been undermined by various influences in the last two hundred years. The workshop the Refore developed and proposed program of ascertainment. The Scope of is to cover the only the South of Sudan includes all the Customary Law regimes With priorities to the following: (a) Mapping (or identification) of all the Customary Law regimes, (b) Ascertainment, recording/documentation of Customary Laws of various ethnic groups, starting with the completely unwritten ones. (c) Updating of documented Customary Law regimes; e.g,Wanh-alel and Fangak, (d) Review, reform, and where possible, harmonization of different Customary Law regimes. The research fields were divided into three regions corresponding to Bahr el Ghazal, Equatorial and Upper Nile respectively. Further Bahr el Ghazal as a research field will have 4 research teams, Equatorial 6, and Upper Nile 4. The Research methodology should be developed with the assistance of experts. However, in respect of the wishes of the southern Sudanese the program was due to start on 2005, but the start were adjourned und the project put on hold because of funding difficulties For more details, see the First Customary Law Work Plan Workshop Held at Nairobi (14ᵗʰ – 16ᵗʰ December 2004.)

3   The majority of social scientists, anthropologists and historians agree that today the Re are about fifty tribes in the region of southern Sudan. Each tribe has developed over time unique customs, practices and beliefs that distinguish them from other tribes. Many have distinct ethnic and language differences, though language divergences are mainly those of dialects rather than fundamental linguistic disparities.

4   The colonial administration, seeking equitable access to adequate pasturage for all tribes, introduced a different system and thus eliminated one of the tribe's two responsibilities.

5   Customary Law is the expression of the customs, beliefs and practices of the people of southern Sudan. The Dinka are over fifty tribes in the region and most have customary law systems, reflecting individual tribal identities. Cited from a Study by Justice Aleu Akechak Jok, LLB, Robert A Leitch, M.BE, Carrie Vandewint, B.Hum M.A. For World Vision International And The South Sudan Secretariat of Legal and Constitutional Affairs March 2004

6   See: Dias, Jurisprudence, p. 246

7   See: John Wuol Makec Customary Law of the Dinka People of Sudan: In Comparison with the Aspects of Western and Islamic Laws, Afro-world Pub. Co., April 1988, P. 22

8   See John Henry Merryman, The Common Law Tradition, p. 23 (2d Ed. 1985). In *R. v Secretary of State For Foreign and Commonwealth Affairs*, [1982] 2 All E.R. 118, Lord Denning said "These customary laws are not written down. They are handed down by tradition from one generation to another. Yet beyond doubt they are well established and have the force of law within the community".

9   Common Law System refers to the legal system within the United Kingdom that largely based on judge-made law (law developed through decisions by judges necessary to decide cases brought before them - called "common law" or case-law) until around the seventeenth century. Each jurisdiction developed its own forms of common law, with Scotland being especially distinct from the rest. Since that time, new laws and law reform have increasingly been brought about through

Acts of Parliament, usually inspired by policies of the Government of the day. Even so, the development of case-law still remains an important source of law. A statement of law made by a judge in a case can become binding on later judges and can in this way become the law for everyone to follow. Whether or not a particular pronouncement (technically called a precedent) by a judge sitting in court when deciding a case does become binding (according to the doctrine of "stare decisis" - stand by what has previously been decided) on later judges depends on two main factors: See: Smith & Baiely The Modern English Legal System, 2. Ed., Sweet & Maxwell, London 1991.

 Peter Orebech and Fred Booelman, the linkage between sustainable development and customary law, p. 12.

10   Peter Orebech and Fred Booelman, the linkage between sustainable development and customary law, p. 12,.

11   When a large section of the populace is in the habit of doing a thing over a very long period, it may become necessary for the courts to take notice of it. The reaction of the people themselves may manifest itself in mere unthinking adherence to a practice, which they follow simply because it is done; or again it may show itself in a conviction that a practice should continue to be observed, because they approve of it as a model of behaviour. The more people follow a practice the greater pressure against non-conformity. But it is not the development of a practice as such, but the growth of a conviction that it ought to be followed that makes it a model for behaviour." Dias, Jurisprudence, 2nd edition., Butterworth, London 1964, p.142

12   Quotes the opinion of Leon Sheleff, University of Tel Aviv, P. 16, The Role of Customary Law in Sustainable Development, Cambridge University Press, 1999.

13

14   John Henry Merryman, Civil Law Tradition: Introduction to the Legal Systems of Western Europe and Latin America, Stanford U.P. February 1970.

15   See: A Manual of Nuer Law, P.P. Howell, Oxford Press, 1970., p. 206

16   Mohamed, El Sheikh Omar, Law of Civil Procedures, 1. Part, P 2.

17   See Section 5 of Civil Justice Act 1983, also previous laws in Sudan recognized custom as source of law e.g. The Chiefs Courts Ordinance 1931 and the Native Courts Ordinance 1932, and The Peoples Local Courts Act 1977

18   According to Sir Henry Maine: a Custom can be a source of Law if it be regarded as conferring legally enforceable rights and if it fulfil following criteria. Time immemorial: It must have existed since 'time immemorial'. A statute fixed this in 1275 as meaning since at least 1189. In practice today claimants usually seek to prove the custom has existed as far back as living memory can go, often as calling the oldest inhabitant as a witness. However, this may not always be sufficient. In a dispute over the right to use local land in some way, for example, if the other side could prove that the land was under water until the seventeenth or eighteenth century the right could not have therefore existed before 1189. .Reasonableness: A legally enforceable custom cannot conflict with fundamental principles of right and wrong, so a customary right to commit a crime, for example, could never be accepted. Certainty and clarity: It must be certain and clear. The locality in which the custom operates must be defined, along with the people to whom rights are granted and the extent of those rights. In Wilson *v* Willes (1806) the tenants of a manor claimed the customary right to take as much turf as they needed for their lawns from the manorial commons. This was held to be too vague, since the Re appeared to be no limit to the amount of turf which could be taken. Locality. It must be specific to a particular geographical area. When a custom is recognized as granting a right, it grants that right only to those specified.

Custom is only ever a source of local law. It must have existed continuously. The rights granted by custom do not have to be exercised continuously since 1189, but it must have been possible to exercise then since then. Exercised as of right: It must have been exercised peaceably, openly and as of right. Customs cannot create legal rights if they are only exercised by permission of someone else. In Mills *v* Corporation of Colchester (1867) it was held that a customary right to fish had no legal force where the right had always depended on the granting of a licence, even though such licences had traditionally been granted to local people on request. Consistency: It must be consistent with other local customs. For example, if a custom is alleged to give the inhabitants of one farm the right to fish in a lake it cannot give another farm the right to drain the lake. The usual course where conflict arises is to deny that the custom has any force, though this is not possible if it has already been recognized by a court. Obligatory: Where a custom imposes a specific duty, that duty must be obligatory- a custom cannot provide that the Lord of the Manor grants villagers a right of way over his land only if he likes them, or happens not to mind people on his land that day. Conformity with a statute: A custom which is in conflict with a statute will not be held to give rise to law; Sir Henry Maine: A Study in Victorian Jurisprudence (Cambridge Studies in English Legal History) von Raymond Cocks, R. C. J. Cocks, und John H. Baker von Cambridge University Pr - 30. September 2004)

19   Legal education started early under the British in what was known as the Gordon Memorial College that eventually became the University of Khartoum. The Faculty of Law of the University of Khartoum was considered one of the best in the African Continent. It admitted about 30 students a year, graduated around 25, most of whom joined the Judiciary, and some the Attorney General's office, increasingly some opting to join the bar and practice privately, and the top in the graduating class were appointed on the Faculty. Over the years, graduates went first to the United Kingdom and later to the United States, including Harvard and Yale Law Schools, for post-graduate studies. See; Short History of Sudan, Mohamed Fadlalla.

20   The criterion of reasonableness arises nearly as often as immemorially and certainty. According to Sir Edward Coke customs must be reasonable or rather taken negatively, they must not be unreasonable. Sir Edward Coke and the Elizabethan Age: Savagery and Civilization in Paris and the South Pacific, 1790-1900 (Jurists-Profiles in Legal Theory), Alice Bullard, Allen D. Boyer, Stanford Uni. Press, December 2000.

21   Section 7 of The Chiefs Courts Ordinance 1931

22   The above-mentioned section provided: A People's local court shall administer he custom prevailing within the local limits of its jurisdiction provided that it is not contrary to justice, morals, or public order. It shall administer the provisions of any other law, the administration of which is authorised by its warrant of establishment or the regulations accompanying the same.

23   John Wuol Makec Customary Law of the Dinka People of Sudan: In Comparison with the Aspects of Western and Islamic Laws, Afro-world Pub. Co., April 1988, P. 26

24   Southern Sudanese and Southern Sudan are excepted from the application of Huddud punishments included by the Islamic inspired Penal Code Act 1991. Customary law inspired penalties are to be applied instead.

25   Comprehensive Peace Agreement CPA of January 9 2005, p. 23.

26   Dar Fur Peace Agreement of Abjua May 5, 2006, Chapter one: power sharing fundamental principles article 1, general principles for power sharing, paragraphs 162, 158.

27   Part One, The State, the Constitution and Guiding Principles, Chapter I, the State and the Constitution, Fundamental Bases of the Constitution of the Interim National Constitution of the Republic of the Sudan 2005.

28   Article 5 (2) Sources of Legislation of the Interim National Constitution of the Republic of the Sudan.

29   Article 5 (2) Sources of Legislation of the Interim National Constitution of the Republic of the Sudan.

30   Among others events to the role of the customary law is as   Project of the Leitner Center for International Law and Justice at Fordham Law School which took place on October 23-24, 2008 Botswana with the title „ The Role of Customary Law in the 21st Century„ sponsored by the organization of African Customary Law.

In the two-.day conference, the participants were invited to present papers on topics related to different areas of customary law. The conference recognizes that Customary law, the traditional law indigenous to a region, continues to regulate many areas of people's lives in Africa.

For example, some African constitutions now enshrine the right to culture and oblige courts to apply customary law where applicable. Elsewhere, constitutional and statutory law have superseded most or all customary law. Yet, even in situations where constitutional law, statutory law and common law have largely superseded it, customary law may nevertheless govern in certain areas, such as family relations. For example, in many places, the requirements for marriage, the rights and duties of husbands and wives, the obligations toward and custody of children, the ownership of property acquired during marriage, and many other aspects of family life are governed by customary law. Moreover, even where conflicting constitutional or statutory law exists, lack of access to legal resources may mean that, as a practical matter, customary law still governs. Finally, the persistence of longstanding expectations and social practices informed by customary law has given rise to many problems in enforcing contradictory statutory law. The conference remarked:

Notwithstanding the significant role customary law continues to play in people's lives, the Re has been a notable lack of research and formal scholarly exchange on the topic. In the following are abstracts of some selected papers:

In a paper from Gordon Woodman who is Emeritus Professor of Comparative Law, Birmingham Law School, University of Birmingham, Birmingham, UK he offers a broad survey of customary law in Africa in historical and contemporary times. From this, he concludes that it is unlikely that the state can totally suppress the observance of customary laws. Indeed, he asserts, attempts at modification alone are likely only to increase the divergence between state law and observed customary laws. These customary laws will continue to change, and although some changes will make their content more similar to that of state laws, considerable differences will remain. Attempts by state legislators or administrators to produce unification, that is, to assimilate customary law to state law will increase the extent of normative conflict (and possibly social conflict also). While it may be desired to move towards harmonisation, that is, to reduce the extent of conflict between state laws and customary laws, Woodman points out that the most effective harmonising measure may be a reduction of the application of received state law and state institutions. Woodman acknowledges common arguments against this approach, referring to the example of gender inequality, which most scholars believe ought to be suppressed by the state. Woodman advocates for a community-led process of harmonisation as a way forward. His paper concludes that the desired changes in customary laws are perhaps more likely to be achieved by schemes to influence the course of social development than by a frontal assault through state legislation".

Abdulmumini Oba (Senior Lecturer, Faculty of Law, University of Ilorin, Ilorin, Nigeria) traces the historical erosion of the substantive and procedural aspects of customary law and asks "What does the future hold for customary law?" Oba insists that one must make a distinction between Islamic law and customary law in this regard. While Islamic law is enjoying a revival across the world and its proponents are committed to the institutionalization of Islamic law as a full-fledged legal system, this is not the case with customary law. It is plain that customary law can no longer go back to its pre-colonial status as a full-fledged legal system. Nevertheless, the author identifies three areas of potential relevancy. First, some norms of customary law would continue to survive particularly in the realms of family law. Secondly, and more importantly, the author thinks that some norms and concepts under customary law will continue to influence the lives of Africans even if those norms and concepts are not consistent with State laws. These include concepts such as ethnic solidarity, collective responsibility, vicarious liability, and the use of juju oaths in informal dispute resolving processes. Thirdly, customary law norms and concepts could be introduced to the European style laws and court systems that are the dominating features of modern nation states in Africa. These could be reflected in the introduction of Alternative Dispute Resolution (ADR) mechanisms such the creation of family courts and simplified court procedures. Concepts depicting African values such the omoluabi (the well-behaved person) concept could also replace tests such as the reasonable man in the law of torts. The African concepts of insult and disgrace would also probably reshape state laws particularly in the treatment of offenders. The paper concludes with a discussion of challenges to the survival of customary law in the twenty-first century. According to Oba, the greatest obstacles are westernized Africans at the helms of the affairs of their countries. See: Customary

Law Revised: AFRICAN CUSTOMARY LAW REVISITED: The Role of Customary Law in the 21st Century October 23-24, 2008 Botswana. Leitner Center for International Law and Justice

31   Similar discussion emerged in relation to customary law in the protection of traditional knowledge in the Anden countries,

The study was launched in regard of the entry into force of the Convention on Biological Diversity (CBD). Since the entry into force of the Convention on Biological Diversity (CBD), the subject of the traditional knowledge of indigenous peoples associated with genetic resources has assumed prominence in international negotiations and has developed in terms of its implementation through three fundamental principles prescribed by the CBD itself, i.e.: the conservation of biodiversity, its sustainable use, and the fair and equitable sharing of benefits resulting from its use. In addition to its treatment within the CBD, in its whole context, the subject of traditional knowledge is also dealt with by the United Nations Conference on Trade and Development (UNCTAD), the United Nations Educational, Scientific and Cultural Organization (UNESCO), the World Intellectual Property Organization (WIPO), the World Trade Organization (WTO), the United Nations Food and Agriculture Organization (FAO), the World Health Organization (WHO), the United Nations Forum on Forests (UNFF), the United Nations Permanent Forum on Indigenous Issues, and other relevant fora. Intense deliberations have generated pressure for the adoption of measures for the protection of traditional knowledge in the international, regional and national spheres. For that reason, various organizations representing indigenous peoples and local communities have signalled the need to ensure that any mechanism for access to genetic resources and associated traditional knowledge must be based on respect for their customary laws and the cultural practices specific to indigenous peoples. In the face of these demands, international negotiations, in particular within the CBD framework and the WIPO Intergovernmental Committee on Intellectual Property and Genetic Resources, Traditional Knowledge and Folklore (IGC), have included in their agendas the treatment of customary law as one of the basic elements for the protection of the traditional knowledge associated with genetic resources and traditional cultural expressions.

Notwithstanding, it is clear that limitations exist with regard to understanding subjects such as the nature, scope, role and jurisdiction of customary law in the conservation and protection of traditional knowledge, which is a very complex subject and still not very clear for many international negotiators. However, for indigenous peoples and local communities it is obvious that their systems of own law are the most appropriate for the protection of their traditional knowledge. At the same time, they recognize the divide between the national law and their systems of own law, since the latter generally lacks adequate recognition in relation to positive national and international law. In order to aid understanding between the systems of customary law (systems of own law) of indigenous peoples and local communities, and those of positive law (the systems codified in the national and international sphere), under the responsibility of WIPO and with the support of the World Conservation Union (IUCN – Regional Office for South America) and the Institute of Advanced Studies of the United Nations University (UNU-IAS), it has been proposed to tackle the subject from a very objective point of view in order to analyze the situation in five Andean countries (Bolivia, Peru, Ecuador, Colombia and Venezuela), and to see how these play an important role in the and sustainable use of genetic resources and in traditional cultural expressions. This regional study has been directed by indigenous experts from the region working in collaboration with non-indigenous legal experts and from other relevant disciplines, in order to identify the tasks to strengthen and/or establish the conditions necessary to ensure an effective relationship between customary law and the systems of positive law at the national, regional and international levels. The proponents of this work know that any study of this nature must be based on an approach which reflects the interests and priorities of indigenous peoples and local communities, whose knowledge and their sui generis protection are the focus of this effort. They have warned the Refore that: Any process which examines the relations between customary law, access to genetic resources and traditional knowledge must be aimed at protecting the ethnic and cultural diversity of indigenous peoples and local communities, for the purpose of guaranteeing their physical and cultural survival, in addition to their well-being and that of humanity as a whole. for this purpose see: Final Report Revised For Wipo Regional

Study In The Andean Countries: "Customary Law In The Protection Of Traditional Knowledge", Rodrigo de la Cruz I. Regional Indigenous Consultant, Quito, November 2006

32   See: Issues in Customary Land Law, Robert D. Cooter, University of California at Berkeley, Robert Cooter. Issues in Customary Land Law, 1989. also The Role of Customary Law in sustainable Development.

A study by the World Vision found that the role and status of women in southern Sudanese society is seen as a reflection of a culture that places a premium on the cohesion and strength of the family as a basis of society and in which the male is the undisputed head of the family and marriage is a means of strengthening the bonds between families an clans within the tribes.

33   A study by the World Vision found that the role and status of women in southern Sudanese society is seen as a reflection of a culture that places a premium on the cohesion and strength of the family as a basis of society and in which the male is the undisputed head of the family and marriage is a means of strengthening the bonds between families an clans within the tribes.

34   The Alternative Dispute Resolution shortly named ADR is a procedure which revived in 1970 in the USA as an alternative methods of conflict- solving before parties to conflict choose the court- way. The ADR involves an independent third person, as mediator who tries to help resolve or narrow the areas of conflict. The use of ADR early in a case can result in the more efficient, cost-effective resolution of disputes with greater satisfaction to the parties. Day, Minh., Alternative Dispute Resolution and Customary Law; Resolving Property Disputes in Post Conflict Nations, A Case Study of Rwanda. Georgetown Immigration Law Journal. Fall 2001. Volume 16 at 235. At 248. 17 Ibid. At 249.

35   Codifications procedure followed in Baher El Ghazal region can also be adopted in further regions in Southern Sudan. In 1975 The Province Commissioner, Sayed Isaiah Kulang invited all chiefs, elders of the people and all heads of Government departments, including Local Government officers, who were experts in customs of this region to a conference to answer a set of questionnaires which prepared by former judge Mr. John Wuol Makec judge of supreme court & head

of the administration of town & rural courts for southern Sudan: The Essentials for the Re of Customary Law in the Southern Sudan by John Wuol Makec, 1992.

36   During the subsequent 21-year civil war, many thousands of Dinka, along with fellow non-Dinka southerners, were killed in the civil war. Dinka built a majority of the rebels of The Sudan People's Liberation led by fomer Dr. John Garang De Mabior, who also belong to Dinka people. The Dinka have also engaged in a separate civil war with the Nuer.

Among the points agreed to in the reconciliation that pending elections, seats in both the Southern Sudan Assembly and the Government of the Southern Sudan are to be divided in a fixed proportion between the SPLM (70%), the NCP (the former NIF) (15%), and "other Southern political forces" (15%). Before his death on 30 July 2005, long-time rebel leader John Garang was the President of Southern Sudan. Garang was succeeded by Salva Kiir Mayardit who was sworn in as first vice president of Sudan on 11 August 2005. Among well-known Dinka are supermodel Alek Wek former NBA player Manute Bol, one of the two tallest players in the league's history current NBA player Luol Deng, Daniel Den, the founder and CEO of the Daniel Deng Non-profit Consulting and Development Corporation (Fiscal Sponsorships and Financial Management).

37   As Abbud's government sought to arabise the south and in 1964 expelled all western missionaries. This led to open civil war in the mid-1960th and the rise of various southern resistance groups, the most powerful of which were the Anya Nya guerrillas, who sought autonomy marking the beginning of a long running north-south civil war. The resulting conflict was known as the civil war and lasted from 1955 to 1972.

In 1972, the Addis Ababa Agreement led to a cessation of the north-south civil war and a degree of self-rule. This led to a ten-year hiatus in the civil war. Under the Addis Ababa Agreement Southern Sudan was given considerable autonomy. In 1983 the civil war was reignited following President Gafar Nimeiri's decision to circumvent the Addis Ababa Agreement. President Gafar Nimeiri attempted to create a Federated Sudan including states in Southern Sudan, which violated the Addis Ababa Agreement, which had granted the South considerable autonomy. The Sudan People's Liberation Army formed in May 1983 as a result. Finally, in June 1983, the Sudanese Government under President Gafar Nimeiri abrogated the Addis Ababa Peace Agreement. The situation was exacerbated after President Gafar Nimeiri went on to implement Sharia Law in September of the same year. The government launched a military campaign in 1991-92 that succeeded in recapturing many military posts that had served as SPLM and SPLA strongholds. The government's success resulted in part from the acquisition of substantial military equipment financed by Iran, including weapons and aircraft bought from China. Another reason for the successes of the government forces was the split that occurred in August 1991 within the SPLA between Garang's Torit fraction (mainly Dinka from southern Al Istiwaia) and the Nasir group (mainly Nuer and other non-Dinka from northern Al Istiwaia). The two groups launched military attacks against each other, the Reby not only destroying their common front against the government but killing numerous civilians. The Nasir group had defected from the main SPLA body and tried unsuccessfully to overthrow John Garang over human rights violations, his authoritarian leadership style, and his favouritism toward his ethnic group, the Dinka. Abortive peace talks with representatives of both groups as well as the government were held in Abuja, Nigeria, in May and early June 1992. In December 1989, former United States president Jimmy Carter had attempted, without success, to mediate peace talks between the government and the SPLA. The Torit fraction sought a secular state and an end to the Sharia; the Nasir group wanted self-determination or independence for southern Sudan. During the talks, both groups agreed to push for self-determination, but when the government rejected this proposal, they decided instead to discuss Nigeria's power-sharing plan. A major basis of southern dissidence was strong opposition to the imposition of the sharia; the SPLA had vowed not to lay down its arms until the Sharia was abrogated. The other source of concern was the fear of northern pressures to arabise the educational system. Al Bashir regime had declared Arabic the language of instruction in the south in early 1992, government offices, and society in general. These fears had led to the civil war, which, with a respite between 1972 and 1983, had been ongoing since 1955. The Bashir government's need for assistance in pursuing the war in the south determined Sudan's foreign policy to a large degree in the 1990s. Al Bashir recognized that the measures taken in the south, which outside observers termed human rights abuses, had alienated the West. Historically, the West had been the source of major financial support for Sudan. Furthermore, by siding with Iraq in the 1991 Persian Gulf War, Sudan had antagonized Saudi Arabia and Kuwait, principal donors for Sudan's military and economic needs in the preceding several decades. Bashir therefore turned to Iran, especially for military aid, and, to a lesser extent, to Libya. Iranian president Ali Hashemi Rafsanjani visited Sudan in December 1991, accompanied by several Peace talks between the southern rebels and the government made substantial progress in 2003 and early 2004. The civil war went for more than 20 years, resulting in the deaths of 2.2 million and displacing roughly 4.5 million people within Sudan and into neighbouring countries. It damaged Sudan's economy and led to food shortages, resulting in starvation and malnutrition. The lack of investment during this time, particularly in the south, meant a generation lost access to basic health services, education, and jobs. The peace was consolidated with the official signing by both sides of the Naivasha treaty on 9th of January 2005, granting Southern Sudan autonomy for six years, to be followed by a referendum about independence. It created a co-vice president position and allowed the north and south to split oil equally, but also left both the North's and South's armies in place. John Garang, the south's elected co-vice president died in a helicopter crash on August 1st, 2005, three weeks after being sworn in. This resulted in riots, but the peace was eventually able to continue. Short History of Sudan by Mohamed H., Dr. Fadlalla, iUniverse, NY, USA, 2004

38   *Kon nei te naadh* : "we are the people of the people" See E.E. Evans-Pritchard , The Nuer: A Description of the Modes of Livelihood and Political Institutions of a Nilotic People, Oxford University Press 1940, p. 3

39   Although Shilluk and Zande tribes and their customary laws do not fall within the study- scope of this book but it is unfair to ignore them as they are significant part of Southern Sudanese tribes.:

The Shilluk (also known as Collo), were mainly settled in a limited, uninterrupted area along the west bank of the Bahr al Jabal, just north of the point where it becomes the White Nile proper. A few live on the eastern bank. With easy access to fairly good land along the Nile, they rely much more heavily on cultivation and fishing than the Dinka and the Nuer, and have fewer cattle. The Shilluk have truly permanent settlements and do not move regularly between cultivations and cattle camps. Unlike the larger groups, the Shilluk, in the Upper Nile, have traditionally been ruled by a single politico-religious head (Reth), believed to become at the time of his investiture as king the representative, if not the reincarnation, of the mythical hero Nyiking, putative founder of the Shilluk. The administrative and political powers of the Reth have been the subject of some debate, but his ritual status is clear enough: his health is believed to be closely related to the material and spiritual welfare of the Shilluk. It is likely that the territorial unity of the Shilluk and the permanence of their settlements have contributed to the centralization of their political and ritual structures. In the late 1980s, the activities against the SPLA by the armed militias supported by the government seriously alienated the Shilluk in Malakal. Nilote is a collective name for many of the peoples living on or near the Bahr al Jabal and its tributaries. The term refers to people speaking languages of one section of the Nilotic sub-branch of the eastern Sudanese branch of Nilo-Saharans and sharing a myth of common origin. They are marked by physical similarity and many common cultural features. Many have a long tradition of cattle keeping, including some for whom cattle were no longer of practical significance.

The Azande are people of north central Africa, the word Azande means the people who possess much land, and refers to their history as conquering warriors. . Their number is estimated by various sources at between 1 and 4 million. They live primarily in the northern part of Democratic Republic of the Congo, in southwestern Sudan, and in the southeastern Central African Republic. The Congolese Azande live in the province of Upper Zaire; the Sudanese Azande live along the shores of the Uele River, and the Central African Azande live in the districts of Rafaï, Zémio, and Obo. They speak an Adamawa-Ubangi language, and most practice a traditional animist religion. Their beliefs revolve mostly around magic, oracles and witchcraft. Witchcraft is believed to be an inherited substance in the belly, which lives a autonomous life performing bad magic on the person's enemies. A witch can sometimes be unaware of his/her powers and can accidentally strike people to whom the witch wishes no evil. Because it's always present the Re are several rituals connected to protection and cancelling of witchcraft, performed almost daily. The Azande emerged in the eighteenth and nineteenth centuries when groups of hunters, divided into aristocrats and commoners, entered the north-eastern part of present-day Zaire (and later south-western Sudan) and conquered the peoples already the Re. Although the aristocrats provided ruling kings and nobles, they did not establish an inclusive, centralized state. Further smaller groups are: Fertit, Anyuak, Murle, Taposa, Latuka, Pari, Acholi, Bari, Pajulu, Kuku, Kakwa, Nyamgwara and Mundari.

The Fertit is a significant minority ethnic group with tribal areas in Western Bahr El Ghazal, cantered on the two counties of Wau and Raja. Their communities are agriculturalist and sedentary. The Fertit are made up of a number of tribes, Balanda, Ndogo, Golo, Kreish, Yulu and Bongo. Their language is distinct and their customs, practices and customary laws reflect their agriculturalist ethos. Like the Zande, the Fertit use money as the currency of customary law actions.

The Anyuak people are a single ethnic group with tribal areas in Eastern Upper Nile and southern Ethiopia. Their language is distinct and for many generations they were cattle owners. Conflict between Anyuak and Nuer has resulted in the Anyuak turning to agriculture as a basis for their economy. Thus their customs, practices and customary laws reflect their agriculturalist lifestyle. The use of special beads known as 'dimoi' as currency in customary law issues, particularly 'bride wealth' is a unique feature of the Anyuak. The practice is in decline and money is more commonly used for such transactions.

The Murle and Taposa are the larger and best known of a group of tribes, which inhabit eastern Equatorial. These tribes, comprising, Murle, Jiye, Taposa, Boya, Didinga, Ngalam and Nyangatum are bound by geography, socio-economics (all are cattle-based societies) and language (though each has their own dialect). The relationship between the tribes, particularly the Murle and Taposa has always been stormy. Conflict, invariably over cattle rustling, is a common state. The tribal areas are notorious for their disregard of 'government' whether British colonial, GoS or SPLA/M. Moreover, frequent forays across the border into Kenya to steal cattle from the Turkana and their reputation for acts of banditry along the Kenyan/Sudanese border, have earned the tribes and the region a reputation for lawlessness. The establishment of law and order in the region has been a priority for SPLA/M and the establishment of their headquarters in Kapoeta County is a significant step in this process. These issues notwithstanding, the Re exists a strong system of customary law shared by the tribes, which has acted as an instrument for reconciliation between them and a means of communication and dialogue during the years of civil war.

The Latuka, Pari and Acholi are the major tribes of a tribal group which inhabits south-eastern Equatorial and across the border into Uganda. Other tribes include Lokoya, Lango, Madi and Lopit. The Re are language differences but a commonality of dialects provides a lingua franca for the communities. All are agriculturalists. Their customs and practices differ in some respects but the Re are sufficient commonalities to provide a compatible system of customary laws.

The Bari, Pajulu, Kuku, Kakwa, Nyamgwara and Mundari. are a number of tribes inhabiting the southern regions of Western Equatoria, bordering on DRC, Their small size, common language and socio-economic status (all are agricultural communities) provide sufficient commonality of customs and practices to enable a compatible system of customary laws.

The Maridi and Mundiri inhabit the western Equatorial region which also home to a group of tribes, classified by geographic region. They include the tribes of Moru, Mundu, Avokaya, Baka and Makaraka. The tribes are agriculturalists and have a commonality of language with differing dialects. Their customs and practices allow for a compatible system of customary laws. See: A Study of Customary Law in Contemporary Southern Sudan, Study by Justice Aleu Akechak Jok, LLB Robert A Leitch, M.BE, Carrie Vandewint, B.Hum M.A. For World Vision International and The South Sudan Secretariat of Legal and Constitutional Affairs, March 2004, p 18-19. and Short History of Sudan, by Mohamed Fadlalla.

40   The natural law theory argues that some rules objectively existing in the nature also are source of law, while legal positivism argues that only the rules made by sovereignty can be the sources of law. See Finnis, John. 1980. *Natural Law and Natural Rights*. Oxford: Clarendon Press., Kainz, Howard P. 2004. *Natural Law: an Introduction and Re-examination*. Open Court. ISBN 0-8126-9454-6.

41   John Wuol Makec Customary Law of the Dinka People of Sudan: In Comparison with the Aspects of Western and Islamic Laws, Afro-world Pub.Co., April 1988, p 32.

42   Such rule of Evidence described in Dinka language as (ke long dan theer) , see John Wuol Makec Customary Law of the Dinka People of Sudan: In Comparison with the Aspects of Western and Islamic Laws, Afro-world Pub. Co., April 1988, p 32.

43   Among the Dinka of South Sudan, banybith (spearmasters or Master of Fishing Spear) have a special place as providers of a range of treatment for health-related conditions. Their role has not been significantly challenged by the arrival of 'Western' medicine.

44   John Wuol Makec Customary Law of the Dinka People of Sudan: In Comparison with the Aspects of Western and Islamic Laws, Afro- world Pub.Co., April 1988, p 33

45   Which refers to all-pervading deity associated with the sky and present in all things, sometimes referred to as creator. See; P.P. Howell, page 204, A Manual of Nuer Law.

46   John Wuol Makec Customary Law of the Dinka People of Sudan: In Comparison with the Aspects of Western and Islamic Laws, Afro-world Pub. Co., April 1988.

47   John Wuol Makec Customary Law of the Dinka People of Sudan: In Comparison with the Aspects of Western and Islamic Laws, Afro- world Publication .Co., April 1988.

48   John Wuol Makec Customary Law of the Dinka People of Sudan: In Comparison with the Aspects of Western and Islamic Laws, Afro- world Publication .Co., April 1988.

49   There are, however, reports of interference in the application of both customary and statutory law and intimidation of civil courts by

the military. See: Customary Law in the Cross- Fire of Sudan's War, p. 130.

50   Among international and foreign organizations contributed to the peace process and after that to training and qualifying jurist for after – war- period in Southern Sudan is also Max- Planck- Institute in Germany, which started series of projects on 2002 and still running, for more details. http://www.mpil.de/ww/de/pub/forschung/

forschung_im_detail/glob_wisstransf/sudan_peace_projekt.cfm

51   See: Wuol Makec, John., The Essentials for the Reinstatement of Customary Law in the Southern Sudan. The Sudanese Judgment and Precedents Encyclopedia. Sudan Judiciary, Khartoum. Also see: John Wuol Makec Customary Law of the Dinka People of Sudan: In Comparison with the Aspects of Western and Islamic Laws, Afroworld Pub.Co., April 1988.

52   The following example according to John Wuol Makec illustrates how such goods- exchange take place by Dinka: "For example (A) may take, property or a cow from (B) on credit and promise that he will in a future period deliver to B" a similar property or cow. B may demand a guarantee for the repayment of debt from (A), "A "will be required to put into the possession of" B" some other property or cow as a guarantee or security If" A "fails afterwards to discharge the debt or loan as agreed the property held as a security will be appropriated by (B). This system is common among the Nilotics. In these circumstances, " B " holds the security as a trustee and he is under duty to exercise reasonable care for the safety of this property otherwise, if he disposes of such property for his own purpose without consent from (A) or he loses this property through his negligence or the negligence of his representative, he will be liable for a breach .of trust. The other example of these rules is a system which corresponds with the system of lien. The Dinka call it" muok" A person who has done the repair of a thing or has done work on a given property that belongs to another on payment is entitled to retain its possession until such payment has been done. Again while he retains the possession of the property before the payment has been made, he is a trustee and is bound to exercise reasonable care for its safety. More examples could be cited but the Re is no space and time" John Wuol Makec Customary

Law of the Dinka People of Sudan: In Comparison with the Aspects of Western and Islamic Laws, Afro-world Pub. Co., April 1988.

53   In case of theft, a thief can be ordered to pay two or three times of value of the stolen object, by adultery, the accused has to pay heavy compensation on the husband or trustee of a married woman: John Wuol Makec Customary Law of the Dinka People of Sudan.

54   The Act comprises the customary law of three groups: Dinka, Luo and Fertit. See Appendix: sections. 7, 83 and 146 provide: "The provisions of this Regional Code shall apply throughout the Region of Bahr El Ghazal to the following types of persons and situation...." The sections then proceed to define the type of persons and situations on which the laws apply. However, despite the enactment of the rules as a statute, these rules, which regulate personal status, can still apply to community members outside the Region of Bahr El Ghazal.. The customary laws of Bahr-el-Ghazal, which had been codified under the leadership of the then Speaker of Bahr-el-Ghazal regional assembly, John Wuol Makec, before the commencement of the war, remained in force under the name 'The Re-Statement of Bahr-el-Ghazal Region Customary Law (Amendment) Act 1984.

55   Compare the situation in Islamic law; polygamy is also recognized in Sharia but the number of women married to at same time is limited to four. Although comparison as to the situation in Sharia is beyond the scope of this study, but it worth mentioning that even some Islamic inspired laws like in Turkey prohibit polygamy.

56   John Wuol Makec Customary Law of the Dinka People of Sudan: In Comparison with the Aspects of Western and Islamic Laws, Afro-world Pub. Co., April 1988, P.56. also; Survey of African Marriage and Family Life by Arthur Phillips, AMS, Pr Inc June 1974

57   John Wuol Makec Customary Law of the Dinka People of Sudan: In Comparison with the Aspects of Western and Islamic Laws, Afro-world Pub.Co., April 1988, P 56.

58   John Wuol Makec Customary Law of the Dinka People of Sudan: In Comparison with the Aspects of Western and Islamic Laws, Afro-world Pub.Co., April 1988, P 59.

59   John Wuol Makec Customary Law of the Dinka People of Sudan: In Comparison with the Aspects of Western and Islamic Laws, Afro-world Pub.Co., April 1988, P 60.

60   The Restatement of Baher el- Ghazal Region Customary Act 1984, Section 12(i)

61   Compare the situation in Islamic Law regarding consent of to be married woman: John Wuol Makec Customary Law of the Dinka People of Sudan: In Comparison with the Aspects of Western and Islamic Laws, Afro-world Pub. Co., April 1988, P 62.

62   The Restatement of Baher el- Ghazal Region Customary Act 1984, sections 26, 27 and 29.

63   The Restatement of Baher el- Ghazal Region Customary Act 1984, Section 21(a),(b). .

64   The most reliable opinion related to reason behind bride-gift says: The marriage payment can be regarded as an indemnity or compensation given by the bridegroom or his family to the bride's family for the loss of their daughter... In societies in which the marriage payment is of considerable value it is commonly used to replace the daughter by obtaining a wife for some other member of the family, usually a brother of a woman who has been lost. Reading in African Law, Vol. II, Frank Cass, London, 1970, p. 86. Survey of African Marriage and Family, Oxford University Press, 1955.

65   Although ghost- marriage is an obligation on the kinship, this obligation is not fulfilled in respect of or dead. A manual of Nuer law, Paul Philip Howell.(Reprint) Publ. for the International African Institute, London : Oxford Univ. Pr., (1970) P. 76. Survey of African Marriage and Family, Oxford University Press, 1955.

66   See Section 1.1.3. Bridewealth and follwoing.

67   A manual of Nuer law, Paul Philip Howell.(Reprint) Publ. for the International African Institute, London : Oxford Univ. Pr., (1970). Survey of African Marriage and Family Life, Arthur Phillips, Oxford University Press, 1953.

68   A manual of Nuer law, Paul Philip Howell.(Reprint) Publ. for the International African Institute, London : Oxford Univ. Pr., (1970)..

Survey of African Marriage and Family Life, Arthur Phillips, Oxford University Press, 1953

69   A manual of Nuer law, Paul Philip Howell.(Reprint) Publ. for the International African Institute, London: Oxford Univ. Pr., (1970). Survey of African Marriage and Family Life, Arthur Phillips, Oxford University Press, 1953.

70   This includes a goat or two, a spear, a fish - spear, a ring and other offerings. See: A manual of Nuer law, Paul Philip Howell.(Reprint) Publ. for the International African Institute, London : Oxford Univ. Pr., (1970) P.95

Survey of African Marriage and Family Life, Arthur Phillips, Oxford University Press, 1953.

71   John Wuol Makec Customary Law of the Dinka People of Sudan: In Comparison with the Aspects of Western and Islamic Laws, Afro-world Pub. Co., April 1988, P 80.

72   John Wuol Makec compares it with the case of declaring marriage nullified in Common Law Customary Law. See: Customary of the Dinka People of Sudan: In Comparison with the Aspects of Western and Islamic Laws, Afro-world Pub. Co., April 1988, p 81.

73   The most cases before court are related to private divorce which parties later requested court involvement to solve dispuate: See Customary Law of the Dinka People of Sudan: In Comparison with the Aspects of Western and Islamic Laws, Afro-world Pub.Co., April 1988 Adut Puouwak v. Tiera and Maguek Atony v. Marial Dorin and others:, John Gum v. Martin Makuet Abol , Macuny Mulok v. Sol. Amiro   p 82 - 85.

74   Thkmer and others v. Malual Cindut, Maguek Atony v. Murial and others, the above mentioned reference p. 88, 89.

75   Application and procedure of Dinka Law upon such disputes show similarity to the application of Venda Law, See: Readings in African Law, Vol. II, Frank Cass, London, 1970, p. 243. and J.J. Van Warmedo, W.M.D. Bhophi, Venda Law in Readings in African Law, Vol. II, Frank Cass, 1970, p 243. John Wuol Makec Customary Law of the Dinka People of Sudan: In Comparison with the Aspects of Western and Islamic Laws, Afro-world Pub. Co., April 1988, P 90.

76   In Buol Yuol v. Irneo Dut: The province court of Baher el Ghazal pronounced decision upon divorce but it was silent as to the payment of *"aruok"* cattle to the relative of the divorced woman. A kinsman of the wife claimed before that court for *aruok* cattle. The court-obliged defendant to pay four cows and one bull as *aruok* or an equivalent value in money on the maternal uncles otherwise the child must be delivered to the plaintiff. See: John Wuol Makec Customary Law of the Dinka People of Sudan, p 98

It is important to emphasize again the difference between *arueth* cattle, which stands for bride-wealth and *arouk* cattle, which stands for each child born during the marriage.

77   A Manual of Nuer Law, P 137. Survey of African Marriage and Family Life, p 113

78   According to some sources ten cattle is the least number to be delivered for two children. See: A Manual of Nuer Law, P 137.

79   See: A Manual of Nuer Law, P 138, also: Majok Depyang v. Cah Macoat (Dok Nuer Case), Carok Jyath v. Won Teang (Dok Nuer Case), Kwic Thowath v. Ngothek Deng (Bul Nuer Case), Cuol Dak v. Liep Balow (Dok Nuer Case).

80   A Manual of Nuer Law, Ps 142- 143 and. Survey of African Marriage and Family Life, p 190-193.

81   A Manual of Nuer Law, Ps 142- 143 and. Survey of African Marriage and Family Life, p 190-193.

82   See: Dang Keng v. Nyag Rih: Dang married Nyag's sister. The Re were no children, and Dang demanded a divorce on grounds of his wife's barrenness. This was refused by the court in the first instance but was allowed two years later by the court of appeal.

83   Compare the situation in Islamic Law. Although Islamic based laws of Arabic and Islamic countries contain different rules as until which age a child should remain in the custody of his mother, but the are all unified as to the rule, that a young child remains by his mother: the differences regarding age are not only related to the different laws of Islamic and Arabic countries but also to which Islamic school is followed in the mean country: for example, in Sudan, Islamic law provides that a daughter remains in her mothers custody till she reaches nine years and

a son till he reaches seven years of age. The Egyptian family law, which follows the doctrine of Hanafi School, provides that a child should remain in custody of his mother till ten years of age for son and twelve for a daughter. See: Mohamed Fadlalla, Islamic Marriage and Child Law in Sudan.

84   Compare The Situation in German Family Law, which differentiates between "Gütergemeinschaft": in which spouses put all during marriage gained property together und "Gütertrennung" by which each spouse would keep his during marriage acquired property for himself. See: Mohamed Fadlalla, Islamic Family and Child Law in Sudan Compared with German Family Law, p. 83-85.

85   Except such ornaments like guen- jang and tung- akoon which is carved elephant tusk which belongs to husband unless wife has brought them in the marriage-home. See: John Wuol Makec Customary Law of the Dinka People of Sudan: In Comparison with the Aspects of Western and Islamic Laws, Afro-world Pub. Co., April 1988.

86   Manual of Nuer law, Paul Philip Howell.(Reprint) Publ. for the International African Institute, London: Oxford Univ. Pr., (1970). P 149-150. Survey of African Marriage and Family Life, Arthur Phillips, Oxford University Press, 1953. P. 195.

87   Manual of Nuer law, Paul Philip Howell.(Reprint) Publ. for the International African Institute, London : Oxford Univ. Pr., (1970). Survey of African Marriage and Family Life, Arthur Phillips, Oxford University Press, 1953. P. 195

88   Return of material property: Wiea Nyah v. Nyadoiny Yol and Gac Cuoö v. Mathot Cung in p. 151 of Manual of Nuer law, Paul Philip Howell.(Reprint) Publ. for the International African Institute, London : Oxford Univ. Pr., (1970). Survey of African Marriage and Family Life, Arthur Phillips, Oxford University Press, 1953.

89   John Wuol Makec Customary Law of the Dinka People of Sudan: In Comparison with the Aspects of Western and Islamic Laws, Afro-world Pub. Co., April 1988, P 122

90   Section 63 of The Restatement of Baher el- Ghazal Region Customary Act 1984, John Wuol Makec Customary Law of the Dinka

People of Sudan: In Comparison with the Aspects of Western and Islamic Laws, Afro-world Pub. Co., April 1988, P 123

91   See: Chief Majak Malok Akot v. Akot Nyadiyiel and others.

In the above-mentioned case Nyadiyiel together with others, collaborators stole a bull from Majak's cattle camp. They sold the stolen cattle in a markt in Rumbek to Chief Yiegi dongrin who had no knowledge that it was stolen. Chief Majak Malok Akot identified his property in the possession of Chief Yiegi dongrin. In following procedure wrongdoer were arrested and convicted and cattle was returned to legal owner. The court's decision was based on the fact that although third party acquired property in good faith against payment, ownership still vested in legal owner "first party" and thus stolen property must be returned to him, since legal owner can not be deprived his ownership right through illegal theft act. The innocent third party has the right to recover payment from second part.

92   Majok Akok v. Dut Ager and Riak Ager CS/172/70, in this case, the Plaintiff had previous knowledge that he is acquiring stolen property.

93   Col. Mathet v. Mathiang Yang

94   Section 53 of The Restatement of Baher el- Ghazal Region Customary Act 1984,.

John Wuol Makec Customary Law of the Dinka People of Sudan: In Comparison with the Aspects of Western and Islamic Laws, Afro-world Pub. Co., April 1988, P 127

95   See: Moses Abaker v. Issa Makuac, RMRY/Civ, App/24/77" The Marriage had been concluded according to the Dinka customary law. The bridewealth was paid in money and distributed between wife's relatives. After divorced, the husband claimed recovery of bridewealth.. it was held that the declaration of divorce resulted in the reversion of title to the bridewealth money to the husband. The third parties received parts of bridewealth were ordered to return money to the husband.

96   In Marial Reec and Manhom Col v. Meen Makerlil [RMRY/ Civ/App/34/77] The wife of Meen Makerlil and the sister of Manhom Col were friends. As a token of friendship, Meen Makerlil and his

wife gave property (a cow) to Manhom Col and his sister. Manhom Col married the daughter of Marial Reec (the Appellant). Some of the offspring of the cow were transferred to Marial Reec as part of the bridewealth and other offspring remained by Manhom Col. Later, the wife of Meen Makerlil died and he decided to terminate the marriage. He also revoked the gift because Manhom Col did not, on reciprocal basis, pay him a cow as a gift of friendship. It was held that since gift was revoked, the title to original cow together with its offspring reverted to Meen Makerlil

97   In Mabur Abiel v. Makur Dhuol /RMRY/Civ. App/7/77 Makur Dhoul "the defendant " illegally acquired by theft a cow that belong to Mabour Abiel "the plaintiff". The defendant alleged founding the cow somewhere and took it as ownerless lost property. In spite of lacking, provide evidence by defendant of those allegations he won first instance decision of the regional court. In the second instance trail, the court of appeal found that the plaintiff and appellant already presented enough evidence to proof his ownership for the cow as well as for its offspring where the defendant neither in first nor in second instance could do.

98   Section 51 of The Restatement of Baher el- Ghazal Region Customary Act 1984 provides: Where a person, who owns property, dies intestate the following persons

shall be the heirs or successors:

(1) Wife and children;

(2) Parents or brothers, if the Re are no wife and children.

99   Section 52 of The Restatement of Baher el- Ghazal Region Customary Act 1984 provides: Where the person who dies intestate has no wife, children, parents nor brothers, his paternal uncle, if no maternal uncle, shall hold the possession of the property as a trustee. He shall use this property in remarrying a woman for the deceased and transfer any balance of the said property to the deceased's newly married woman, who shall also hold it partly as a trustee for her children

100   An Example of this cited in the Customary Law of the Dinka People of Sudan: In Comparison with the Aspects of Western and

165

Islamic Laws, Afro-world Pub. Co., April 1988, P 155 by John Wuol Makec.

101   The Problems regarding the nature of individual right's to land were discussed by Dr. Francis Deng, in Property and Value- Interplay among the Nilotes, 1965, SLJR pp.- 592- 595

102   The Customary Law of the Dinka People of Sudan: In Comparison with the Aspects of Western and Islamic Laws, Afro-world Pub. Co., April 1988, P 157.

103   Dr. Francis Deng, Property and Value- Interplay among the Nilotes, 1965, SLJR pp.- 592- 595.

104   File No. BP/6-B1,p. 5

105   This is the opinion of Dr. Francis Deng, Property and Value- Interplay among the Nilotes, 1965, SLJR pp.- 592- 595. Also see: The Customary Law of the Dinka People of Sudan: In Comparison with the Aspects of Western and Islamic Laws, Afro-world Pub. Co., April 1988, P 170

106   See: The Customary Law of the Dinka People of Sudan: In Comparison with the Aspects of Western and Islamic Laws, Afro-world Pub. Co., April 1988, P 172.

107   Nuer use the expression "dun- da" which stands for "my thing" and "nyin-ke " which stands for "his things" See: p. 178 of A manual of Nuer law, Paul Philip Howell.(Reprint) Publ. for the International African Institute, London : Oxford Univ. Pr., (1970).

108   A Manual of Nuer Law, Paul Philip Howell.(Reprint) Publ. for the International African Institute, London : Oxford Univ. Pr., (1970), p 184

109   Paul Philip Howell, p 185

110   Paul Philip Howell, p 185

111   Section 66 of the Restatement of Baher El-Gahzal Region Customary Law Act (amended) 1984   provides: Any person who retains possession of a cow or other property as 'amuk' (pledge) or any property for the work done on it (lien) is bound to exercise reasonable care for it. If such a cow or property perishes or disappears through his negligence or the negligence of his successor or agent, he is bound to

pay damages to the owner, in case of the property held for work done on it: and in case of amuk', the property or cow which has perished or disappeared in his possession through such negligence shall be deemed as full satisfaction of his claim against the debtor.

112   Case of trust called "kuei"See: e Customary Law of the Dinka People of Sudan: In Comparison with the Aspects of Western and Islamic Laws, Afro-world Pub. Co., April 1988, p.188.

113   See: Col Mathet v. Mathiang Yang and Agree Miith: it was held that according to the terms of the agreement the plaintiff was entitled only to one heifer. The term of the agreement could not be varied by passage of time. The first defendant was ordered to pay only a heifer, as he originally promised to the plaintiff. Case of trust called "kuei"See: Customary Law of the Dinka People of Sudan: In Comparison with the Aspects of Western and Islamic Laws, Afro-world Pub. Co., April 1988, p.189.

114   Section 79 of the Restatement of Baher El-Gahzal Region Customary Law Act (amended) 1984 provides: Damages to properly : When the property of anyone is damaged by (i) a cow or bull, or (ii) a goat or a he-goat, or (iii) a sheep or a ram, which belongs to another person, the owner of the property is entitled to obtain damages from the owner of such animal in the form of money calculated according to the degree of damage done

115   See: Customary Law of the Dinka People of Sudan: In Comparison with the Aspects of Western and Islamic Laws, Afro-world Pub. Co., April 1988, p.195.

116   Section 80 provides: (When a cow or bull or goat or he-goat or sheep or ram dies owing to the injury caused, while it was within the owner's premises, by another trespassing or wandering cow or bull or goat or sheep or ram or he-goat that belongs to another person, the animal that inflicted the injury which caused the death shall be awarded to the owner of the animal which has been killed as damages, but no damages shall be awarded if the injury was caused while both animals were wandering outside the premises of their owners or when trespassing in the premises of a third party).

117   The above- mentioned opinion is according to Dr. Francis Deng. See: Customary Law of the Dinka People of Sudan: In Comparison

with the Aspects of Western and Islamic Laws, Afro-world Pub. Co., April 1988, p 199.

118   Section 70 of the Restatement of Baher El-Ghazal Region Customary Law Act (amended) 1984 provides When apuk is payable by killer's relatives of by the whole tribe When two tribes or more enter into a fight and some people get killed on either side, the payment of apuk' to the Relatives of the deceased person or persons shall be confined to the killers and their Relatives, but where the killer is unknown, the tribe involved in the fight against the deceased's tribe is bound to pay apuk or compensation is 30 cows for causing the death of a person. Section 71 of the Re-Statement of Bahr El Ghazal Region Customary Law (Amended) Act 1984 Bahr El-Ghazal Region Act No. 1, 1984 provides: Self- defence is no excuse for avoiding payment of apuk

A person who has caused the death of another is bound with his Relatives on the paternal side to pay apuk of thirty (30) cows to the Relatives of the deceased, although death might have been caused while the killer was exercising the right of self-defence.

119   This dose not mean that Dinka Customary Law and others African Customary Laws do not know such elements. See: Frank Coss, Reading in African Law, London 1970, Vol. 1 p. 165. (The Re is a notion of mens rea in African Law...When people deny that motive, intention, etc, play any part in African Law they seem to be arguing from particular to the general- from the single instance of homicide and its treatment to the whole African Law. They forget that all African Law is neither homicide nor even crime in general, and that the Re are large areas of civil law in which these concepts (.e. motive, intention etc.) are fully regarded by the elders in their adjudication dispute.

120   Section 70 of the Re-Statement of Bahr El Ghazal Region Customary Law (Amended) Act 1984 Bahr El-Ghazal Region Act No. 1, 1984 provides When apuk is payable by killer's relatives of by the whole tribe. When two tribes or more enter into a fight and some people get killed on either side, the payment of apuk to the Relatives of the deceased person or persons shall be confined to the killers and their Relatives. But where the killer is unknown, the tribe involved in the

fight against the deceased's tribe is bound to pay apuk or compensation is 30 cows for causing the death of a person.

121   Section 75 provides; Apuk is ten (10) cows where a person is killed by one who lacks capacity or who is insane, where a person is killed by another who is insane or lunatic, or a child who lacks capacity, the Relatives of the killer arc bound to pay ten (10) cows as apuk to the Relatives of the deceased.

122   Section 74 of the Re-Statement of Bahr El Ghazal Region Customary Law (Amended) Act 1984 Bahr El-Ghazal Region Act No. 1, 1984 provides

Apuk is ten (10) cows when a person is killed through mistake of fact

Where a person kills another through a mistake of fact (rol), he is bound to pay ten (10) cows as apuk to the Relatives of the deceased.

123   Section 76 of the Re-Statement of Bahr El Ghazal Region Customary Law (Amended) Act 1984 Bahr El-Ghazal Region Act No. 1, 1984 provides; Apuk is thirty (30) head of cattle when a relative other than a member of the same family is killed. Where a person intentionally causes the death of his Kinsman other than a member of his family, he is bound to pay thirty (30) head of cattle as apuk to the Relatives of the deceased, unless the members of the deceased's family waive their rights.

124   Section 72 of the Re-Statement of Bahr El Ghazal Region Customary Law (Amended) Act 1984 Bahr El-Ghazal Region Act No. 1, 1984 provides: Apuk and bride-wealth properly payable to the husband's Relatives when killed by his wife If a woman intentionally causes the death of her husband, the marriage is automatically dissolved and the Relatives of the deceased are entitled to obtain apuk cattle together with the cattle they had paid for bride-wealth during the marriage from her Relatives, provided that, if the Re arc children, the deceased Relatives are bound to pay 'aruok' cattle to her Relatives for each child, otherwise her parents or Relatives shall be entitled to take the children

125   Section 77 of the Re-Statement of Bahr El Ghazal Region Customary Law (Amended) Act 1984 Bahr El-Ghazal Region Act No. 1, 1984 provides: Apuk is payable by the husband and his Relatives

if his wife kills another person Where a married woman kills another person, who is not her husband's Kinsman, apuk must be paid to the Relatives of the deceased by her husband and his Relatives. But if the marriage between such a woman and her husband is afterwards dissolved, the husband shall be entitled to recover from her Relatives the cattle he had paid as bride-wealth together with damages for the thirty (30) head of cattle he had paid for the apuk provided that he shall at the same time be bound to settle all other rights claimed against him by her Relatives.

126   Section 73 of the Re-Statement of Bahr El Ghazal Region Customary Law (Amended) Act 1984 Bahr El-Ghazal Region Act No. 1, 1984 provides Bridewealth cattle convertible info apuk cattle when husband kills his wife When a husband intentionally kills his wife, the marriage is dissolved and the cattle which he had paid to her Relatives as bride-wealth cattle shall be converted into apuk cattle, but if the amount of the bridewealth cattle he had paid was less than thirty (30) head of cattle, he and his Relatives arc bound to fill the gap by paying more cattle. However, if the amount of bride-wealth cattle was more than thirty (30) head of cattle, he or his successor is entitled to red over the surplus from the deceased's Relatives, provided that he or his successor shall pay 'aruok' cattle for each child together with the 'arueth' cattle or any rightful claims to the Relatives of the deceased.

127   The word in Nuer language   expresses „to kill" is *nak*, compensation is called *thung* (compare it with *apuk*   in Dinka language)

128   See: p 48 a Manual of Nuer Law.

129   As soon as someone is killed among Nuer, a state of feud, called " ter" begins between the two concerned parties. The concerned parties refer the matter to arbitrator called "Leopard -Skin" who acts as arbitrator in settlement of the feuds. The Leopard- Skin is a chief by the reason of his special association with land and traditionally he may use these powers to intervene in conflict between Nuer community-members. Beside his role as mediator, the Leopard- Skin is concerned with spiritual welfare of the killer as individual.

130   The related Ceremony called „birr" it is to be performed either by the Leopard – Skin himself or one of his relatives.

131   See: p 48 a Manual of Nuer Law.

132   Nuer call it „Thung gwacka"

133   See a Manual of Nuer Law, p 68

134   See a Manual of Nuer Law, p 68

135   See a Manual of Nuer Law. p.70

136   Reading in African Law, p.68 Also See: Dr. Francies Deng, (1965) SLJR, p 538

137   Section 27 of the Reinstatement of Baher El Ghazal Region Customary Law Act 1984 provides: Any Dinka who is not a girl is presumed to be a married woman and any man who commits sexual intercourse with such a woman does so at his own risk. According to Sudan Penal Code, 1983 sections 432, 433 when a woman denies being married in the moment of the sexual intercourse and the Re was no other possibility nor reason cause the man to know the fact of her being married. In such a case, only the woman alone is hold responsible for adultery. This responsibility is based on her knowledge of the fact of her being married (the offence of adultery is committed by a man if he knows or has reasons to believe that the woman is married at the time of sexual intercourse between her and him.) replaced by section 146 (4) of Sudan Penal Code Act 1991.

138   The number of cattle payable as compensation "akor" is determined by Section 28 When a man commits adultery with a married woman, he shall pay six cows and one bull to the husband or his successor as 'akor' or 'aruok' and no penalty may be passed against him by the Local Court, but if he has no cattle to pay as 'akor', he shall be punished with imprisonment or fine or with both as prescribed by the Sudan Penal Code.

139   Section 29 of the Reinstatement of Baher El Ghazal Region Customary Law Act 1984 provides: When a married woman commits adultery for a second time with another man after the 'akor' cattle have been paid for the first act of adultery, the husband or his successor or trustee is not entitled to claim any 'akor' cattle again, but the man who

commits the offence shall be punished with imprisonment or fine or both in accordance with the provisions of the Sudan Penal Code.

140 Section 31 of the Reinstatement of Baher El Ghazal Region Customary Law Act 1984 provides:: Whenever a woman commits adultery with a relative of her husband who has contributed a cow or some cows during her marriage as part of the bridewealth, the relative who commits the offence is only bound to pay a cow to the husband or his successor or trustee as 'awec', but if such relative never paid any cow or some cows as his contribution to the bridewealth, he is bound to pay six (6) cows and one bull as 'akor' (or 'aruok') to the husband or his successor.

141 Section 30 of the Reinstatement of Baher El Ghazal Region Customary Law Act 1984 provides:: The husband, or if he is dead, his successor is the only competent party to sue in the case of adultery

142 Section 33 of the Reinstatement of Baher El Ghazal Region Customary Law Act 1984 provides; when a man whose wife has committed adultery with another person elects to divorce her, he is bound to or compelled by the Court to sue the offender in order to obtain "akor" cattle before the divorce or the dissolution of the marriage is granted.

143 Section 32 of the Reinstatement of Baher El Ghazal Region Customary Law Act 1984 provides: The child who is the product of a sexual intercourse between a married woman and another man belongs to the legal father. But, if the legal father elects to divorce his wife and disowns the child, his wife's Relatives will be entitled to have the child. When a husband is compellable to sue for 'Akor' cattle. When a man whose wife has committed adultery with another person elects to divorce her, he is bound or compelled by the Court to sue the offender in order to obtain 'akor' cattle before the divorce or the dissolution of the marriage is granted.

144 Section 32 of the Reinstatement of Baher El Ghazal Region Customary Law

145 This is the case among the majority of the Nuer tribes west of the Nile and Baher al Zaraf region. They consider that if a child is born of an adulterous act, then all cattle paid previously as compensation must be returned by husband with the exception of "yang kule" the

reason therefore is unclear, one may think, it is because the adulterer has done the husband a favour in begetting a child on his behalf. See: a Manual of Nuer Law, p 156.

146   Deng Kac v. Nyuon Makwac: Nyuon Makwac Also see: Not Pet v. Gac Nyol and Kwol Biliu v. Cuol Puot

147   See: Tec Nygh v. Kwoiny Kuok

148   See: Tec Nygh v. Kwoiny Kuok

www.ingramcontent.com/pod-product-compliance
Lightning Source LLC
Chambersburg PA
CBHW032006170526
45157CB00002B/574